Religion and American Constitutions

Religion and American Constitutions

Wilber G. Katz

1963 ROSENTHAL LECTURES

Northwestern University School of Law

NORTHWESTERN UNIVERSITY PRESS

Evanston, Illinois

Acknowledgments

IN DEVELOPING THE POSITION taken in these lectures, I have been helped by criticisms from colleagues at The University of Chicago and The University of Wisconsin. I am indebted also to students in my 1963 Seminar on Church and State.

I acknowledge with warm appreciation the many courtesies and hospitality of Dean John Ritchie III, Professor Vance N. Kirby, Professor Willard H. Pedrick, and other members of the Rosenthal Lectures Committee. I am grateful also to Mrs. Sherry K. Bate for her patient and meticulous care through the many revisions of the manuscript.

WILBER G. KATZ

Madison, December, 1963

47523

Contents

I. RELIGION AND THE CONFLICT OF FREEDOMS *1*

II. PUBLIC EDUCATION—THE ESTABLISHMENT OF AMERICAN RELIGION? *31*

III. RELIGIOUS SCHOOLS—THE PRICE OF FREEDOM? *57*

EPILOGUE. NEUTRALITY AS OF JUNE 1963 *89*

vii

I

Religion and the
Conflict of Freedoms

THE UNITED STATES CONSTITUTION, as originally ratified, had only one explicit reference to religion. Its preamble contained no reference to God, and the only article mentioning religion was Article VI, which provided that "no religious test shall ever be required as a qualification to any office . . . under the United States." The Bill of Rights was soon added, however, providing in the First Amendment that "Congress shall make no law respecting an establishment of religion, or prohibiting the free exercise thereof . . ." We shall be concerned also with the provision of the Fourteenth Amendment that "No State shall . . . deprive any person of life, liberty, or property, without due process of law; . . ." As one might expect, the liberty protected by this clause includes religious liberty, and in recent decades the Supreme Court has declared that the Fourteenth Amendment makes applicable to state legislation both of the religion clauses of the First Amendment— the prohibition of laws "respecting an establishment of religion" as well as the "free exercise" clause.

Most state constitutions contain some explicit reference to the Deity, such as that in the Wisconsin preamble which begins, "We, the people of Wisconsin, grateful to Almighty God for our freedom, . . ." Such references are found in constitutions recently drafted as well as in those adopted in the eighteenth and nineteenth centuries. The constitution of Hawaii opens with an expression of gratitude for "Divine Guidance."

State constitutions are also more detailed than the First Amendment in their protection of religious liberty. Here, too, the Wisconsin constitution is typical. It provides that "The right of every man to worship Almighty God according to the dictates of his own conscience shall never be infringed; nor shall any man be compelled to attend, erect or support any place of worship, or to maintain any ministry, against his consent; nor shall any control of, or interference with, the rights of conscience be permitted . . ." [1]

With respect to establishment of religion, the Wisconsin constitution provides that no preference shall "be given by law to any religious establishments or modes of worship . . ." and, like many other constitutions, it adds a specific restriction on the use of public funds: "nor shall any money be drawn from the treasury for the benefit of religious societies, or religious or theological seminaries." The article on education provides that "no sectarian instruction shall be allowed" either in the district schools or in the state university.[2]

"Free exercise" and "no establishment"

Most of the current controversy over the First Amendment has focused upon the prohibition of laws "respecting an establishment of religion." I shall be dealing principally with this clause and only incidentally with the guaranty of "free exercise of religion." Often the same regulation violates both clauses. This was the case with the Maryland constitutional provision that "no religious test ought ever to be required as a qualification for any office . . . other than a declaration of belief in the existence of God." This exception was recently challenged by Roy R. Torcaso, a prominent member of the American Humanist Association, who was refused a commission as Notary Public when he declined to declare his belief in God. The United States Supreme Court unanimously struck down the requirement, holding that it violated the plaintiff's "freedom of belief and religion," and adopting a broad interpretation of the term "religion." [3] In a footnote, Justice Black referred to "religions . . . which do not teach what would generally be considered a belief in the existence of God" and listed as examples Buddhism, Taoism, Ethical Culture, and Secular Humanism.[4] Here, incidentally, the Court appeared to be taking a side in the vigorous dispute among humanists as to whether humanism is a religion or an alternative to religion.[5] But even if Torcaso's position had been interpreted as nonreligious, the result of the case would have been the same, for if religious belief is to be free, freedom of religion must include freedom of religious disbelief. One can hardly take seriously the argument that those who profess no religion cannot appeal to the First Amendment since "this document was solely concerned with religion itself, not its denial." [6]

But the Court in *Torcaso* did not limit its attention to the "free exercise" clause. Much of its opinion was devoted to the "no establishment" provision, which the Court held to forbid government aid to religions which are based on a belief in the existence of God. Justice Black quoted again the oft-quoted paragraph from his opinion in *Everson v. Board of Education*, the decision sustaining the New Jersey provision of bus transportation for parochial schools. Since our concern will be very largely with the meaning and soundness of this paragraph, I shall therefore quote it in full:

The "establishment of religion" clause of the First Amendment means at least this: Neither a state nor the Federal Government can set up a church. Neither can pass laws which aid one religion, aid all religions, or prefer one religion over another. Neither can force nor influence a person to go to or to remain away from church against his will or force him to profess a belief or disbelief in any religion. No person can be punished for entertaining or professing religious beliefs or disbeliefs, for church attendance or non-attendance. No tax in any amount, large or small, can be levied to support any religious activities or institutions, whatever they may be called, or whatever form they may adopt to teach or practice religion.[7]

The establishment clause—legislative history

In 1962 the Supreme Court followed this "no aid to all religions" interpretation of the "no establishment" clause when it held unconstitutional the prescribed use of the "Regents' prayer" in New York public schools.[8] Thereafter, Bishop James A. Pike told the Senate Judiciary Committee that the Court had "distorted" the establishment clause; that Congress should initiate an amendment restating the clause precisely "in terms of the prohibition our Founding Fathers had in mind." He was clear that what the founding fathers had in mind was merely prohibiting "laws respecting the recognition as an established church of any denomination, sect, or organized religious association." These are the words which he suggested should be substituted in the First Amendment.[9]

Advocates of this interpretation of the establishment clause—like advocates of a broad interpretation in terms of church-state separation—have often claimed clear support in the Congressional history of the First Amendment.[10] Those who make these claims, however, are fairly open to the charge of trying to fortify their positions with what Professor Mark DeWolfe Howe has called "a Maginot line of spurious history."[11]

The Congressional history of the establishment clause is tantalizing. A religion amendment was first introduced in the House of Representatives by James Madison. It provided "nor shall any national religion be established."[12] This formula was probably open to Bishop Pike's interpretation as forbidding merely a particular established church. The House, however, substituted the contrasting language of the New Hampshire proposal: "Congress shall make no laws touching religion."[13] But finally the House passed and sent to the Senate a more ambiguous clause worded as a prohibition of "laws establishing religion."[14] In the Senate there were several votes rejecting clauses like Bishop Pike's,[15] and this action is often relied upon as supporting a separationist interpretation of the final wording. But this ignores the fact that six days later the Senate adopted a quite similar version and sent it to a conference commit-tee.[16] This clause forbade any "law establishing articles of faith or a mode of worship." Out of the conference com-mittee came the language substantially as we have it.

What is usually neglected, when inferences are con-fidently drawn from this legislative history, is the fact that one of the problems confronting the draftsmen was the possibility that Congress might interfere with the privileges of particular established churches which remained in a number of states in New England and in the South. A pur-pose to forbid such interference seems clearly behind the New Hampshire formula, "no laws touching religion," which was very close to the wording finally adopted: "no law respecting an establishment of religion." It seems un-deniable that the First Amendment operated, and was in-tended to operate, to protect from Congressional inter-ference the varying state policies of church establishment. The Amendment thus embodied a principle of federalism.

It seems clear, furthermore, that Congress was to keep its hands off *all* local establishment policies and not merely policies of preferential establishment of a particular sect. One of the live alternatives was that, in abandoning an established church, a state might substitute a policy of multiple establishment; that is, equal support for several or conceivably all religious groups. This was a proposal which had had wide support in Virginia and had been de-feated in 1785 only through the influence of Madison's famous *Memorial and Remonstrance*. It seems to me quite untenable that Congress was left free to interfere with a state arrangement of this kind; I cannot therefore agree with Bishop Pike (and his disciple Senator Eastland) that the words "an establishment of religion" referred simply to preference for a particular sect. I would almost agree with President Henry P. Van Deusen of Union Seminary that on this point "there is no doubt" of the intention of the framers of the First Amendment; except that the position which I consider indubitable is the opposite of that which he shares with Bishop Pike.[17]

The more difficult question concerns the limits, if any, which the clause placed upon the power of Congress to legislate concerning religion in areas beyond the authority of any state; for example, in the armed forces, the District of Columbia, and the territories. The legislative history gives little or no basis for an answer—or even for believing that the problem was considered at all. Perhaps the "no establishment" clause was intended *solely* to rule out Congressional action in an area reserved to the states. It might have been thought that the "free exercise" clause was a sufficient basis from which to draw limitations on the power of Congress to affect religion in federal territory. Any attempt to set up an established church in the Northwest Territory, for example, might readily have been held to violate the "free exercise" clause.

Action of the Continental Congress with respect to land grants in this territory shows how vacillating had been the policy with respect to religion. In 1785 a report recommending as general policy the reservation of two sections in each township, one for the maintenance of public schools and the other "for the support of religion," was amended to eliminate the provision for religion.[18] This action Madison reported in a letter to Monroe with great satisfaction.[19] But on July 23, 1787, the Congress adopted a report—presented by a committee of which Madison was a member—authorizing a particular sale of land with the following stipulation: "The lot N29 in each township or fractional part of a township to be given perpetually for the purposes of religion." [20] I am not suggesting, of course, that Madison actually approved such a provision, but only that the sentiment in the Congress was apparently such that Madison thought it inexpedient to raise the question.

The dearth of evidence as to the restrictions imposed by the "no establishment" clause in federal territory means a dearth of evidence as to the meaning with which the clause was "incorporated" (as the phrase goes) into the Fourteenth Amendment. The only thing we really *know* about the original meaning of the "no establishment" clause is that it forbade Congress to disestablish as well as to establish religion. And the Fourteenth Amendment certainly did not extend this prohibition to the states!

RELIGION AND AMERICAN CONSTITUTIONS

No aid to religion—the neutrality principle

The Court is not to be criticized for seeking its own meaning for the "no establishment" clause, but it may, of course, be questioned whether the broad *Everson* rule of "no aid to religion" was a proper meaning to find. It is often argued that Congress could not have intended a "no aid" rule because it aided religion from its very first session by providing for army chaplains. This argument, however, shows a misunderstanding of the "no aid" rule. As I understand it, the rule against aid to all religion is merely a rule of neutrality. In a later passage in the *Everson* opinion, Justice Black said:

> [The First] Amendment requires the state to be neutral in its relations with groups of religious believers and non-believers; it does not require the state to be their adversary. State power is no more to be used so as to handicap religions, than it is to favor them.[21]

and again:

> . . . we must be careful, in protecting the citizens of New Jersey from state-established churches, to be sure that we do not inadvertently prohibit New Jersey from extending its general state law benefits to all its citizens without regard to their religious belief.[22]

These passages—and the opinion as a whole—support the principle of full neutrality, a principle requiring the government to be neutral not only between sects but also between believers and nonbelievers. Provisions for religious services in the armed forces are not aids to religion which violate the neutrality principle. They are not designed to promote religion, but to protect the religious freedom of those whom the government isolates from civilian life.

The neutrality position has been under recurrent attack from two opposite directions. It is attacked, as we have noted, by those like Bishop Pike who urged that government may properly aid religion so long as it does not favor a particular church. But it is attacked also by those who demand strict separation, not mere neutrality. Strict separation is required, they argue, as a means of insulating the government from all demands for aid, an insulation deemed necessary for the protection of both civil and religious liberty and to reduce occasions for religious controversy in civic life. A rule of absolute separation would mean outlawing provisions designed to implement religious freedom, as in the armed forces. It would require also the denial of all aids to religion, even incidental aids which result from measures which are not designed to promote religion and the benefits of which are not limited to religious groups. It was on this separation theory that four justices dissented from the *Everson* parochial school bus decision.

Sunday closing laws

The decisions concerning Sunday closing laws furnish an excellent setting in which to examine further the full neutrality principle and its rivals. As a result of the 1961 decisions (together with one last autumn), three propositions of law have apparently been settled.[23] First, Sunday closing laws are valid if they can be interpreted as directed primarily to a nonreligious end, such as the provision of a uniform day of rest and recreation. Second, merchants who close their places of business on Saturday as a matter of religious duty need not be exempt from a Sunday closing requirement. But third, if they are granted such exemptions, this does not make the legislation invalid as a law respecting an establishment of religion.

The Court was unanimous in its conviction that a closing law would be invalid if enacted to promote religious observance. To sustain the current laws, admittedly religious in their origins, it was necessary to find that they had come to serve primarily secular purposes. This approach was recently criticized with vigor by Dean Erwin Griswold of Harvard Law School. In his opinion, the Court made the cases hard when "they should have been quite easy." [24] The Court's mistake was in taking as too absolute a requirement the "no aid to religion" rule which Justice Black's *Everson* opinion had drawn from the establishment clause. In Dean

Griswold's opinion, the Sunday laws are legitimate as an expression of the religious tradition of the Christian majority and as an effort to support and maintain that tradition. As for the religious or nonreligious minorities, they are not being forced to *do* anything affirmative, and they therefore have no basis for complaint. The minorities are tolerated, and they should be tolerant of the majority and not ask that the majority give up its Christian heritage and tradition. Of course, the Orthodox Jew or Seventh-day Adventist is not asking the majority to give up observing Sunday. The question is whether a religious tradition is to be maintained through the force of the State. The majority tradition of which Dean Griswold asks minorities to be tolerant is the tradition of supporting Sunday observance by punishing those who offend others or tempt others by keeping shops open on Sunday. This has indeed been part of our tradition. Even James Madison apparently did not hesitate in the year of his victories for religious freedom to present to Virginia legislators "A Bill for Punishing . . . Sabbath Breakers." [25] But Madison in other areas was a leader in transforming a policy of toleration into a policy of religious liberty and equality. With all due respect to Dean Griswold, I question whether it shows undue "absolutism" when the Court finds that criminal penalties may no longer be imposed in order to support religious observances.

Justices Brennan and Stewart dissented in two of the cases, voting to protect the freedom of religious minorities by requiring the exemption of those who close their establishments for religious reasons on another day. As Justice Stewart put it, without such exemption the law may compel an Orthodox Jew to choose between his religious faith and his economic survival. "It is a cruel choice . . . this is not something that can be swept under the rug and forgotten in the interest of enforced Sunday togetherness." [26] The majority, however, were unwilling to force exemptions since they create difficulties of administration and, as the Chief Justice said, since they "might cause the Sunday-observers to complain that their religions are being discriminated against" and might tempt some to pretend to have Sabbatarian convictions. "This might make necessary," he warned, "a state-conducted inquiry into the sincerity of the individual's religious beliefs, a practice which a State might believe would itself run afoul of the spirit of constitutionally protected religious guarantees." [27]

The issue of exemptions is a difficult one and its difficulty lends force to Justice Douglas' simple position that Sunday laws are indefensible. He considers it a subterfuge to interpret such laws as secular regulations. They are enacted, he insists, to provide "a coercive spur to the 'weaker brethren.' " [28] And I read his objection as going deeper. Even if a closing law were clearly the result of pressure from business groups rather than from Christian churches, Justice Douglas would still insist that its enforcement aids in promoting religious observance and that all such aids are improper. If this interpretation is correct, he is invoking a strict separation principle. The majority, however, tolerate incidental aids which accrue to religion from measures designed to serve other purposes. They see the "no establishment" clause as requiring no more than neutrality.

It must be conceded that the arguments for strict separation have some force in the Sunday law context. In several states today, state legislatures and municipal councils have before them proposals for closing laws behind which religious groups as well as commercial interests are mobilizing support. Many a legislator would welcome a strict separation doctrine which would protect him from religious pressures by eliminating the possibility of any such legislation. But no one can hope completely to remove religious controversy from public life by interpreting the First Amendment in strict separation terms. Religious views of citizens will necessarily influence—and should influence—their position on many public questions, though there are limits, of course, to the propriety of incorporating into law particular views of religious morality.

It is important to note that religious leaders are among those voicing opposition to Sunday closing laws. For example, a Presbyterian Committee on Church and State has urged that church members should make no efforts to pass or strengthen Sunday laws. "Such efforts," they say, "are not conducive to an effective witness to Jesus Christ, regardless of what motivates them." [29] This recommendation reflects the growing concern of church leaders over the superficial character of the commitment of many church members. "Routine religiosity" is a term often used by such critics. Peter Berger (whose book *The Noise of Solemn Assemblies* was recommended in the Presbyterian report) says that the trouble is religious establishment and that the way to revive prophetic vigor in the churches is disestablishment. He is not speaking technically of legal establishment but of a general cultural establishment in which the churches too often contribute no prophetic criticism but merely a religious aura to sanctify the American way of life.

Religious exemptions

I have already noted that when Sunday closing laws grant exemption to those who close on another day because of religious scruples, an additional constitutional question arises. Such an exemption was once stricken down by the Louisiana court as discriminatory. The court said, "Before the constitution, Jews and Gentiles are equal; by the law they must be treated alike, and the ordinance of a City Council which gives one sect a privilege which it denies to another, violates both the constitution and the law, and is therefore null and void." [30] In one of the 1961 cases, however, Chief Justice Warren's majority opinion noted that "A number of States provide such an exemption" and commented that "this may well be the wiser solution to the problem." [31] And Justice Frankfurter said in his concurring opinion, "However preferable, personally, one might deem such an exception, I cannot find that the Constitution compels it." [32]

In 1962 a Kentucky exemption of this type was attacked by a nonsabbatarian under the "no establishment" clause. The state court held, however, that the exemption did not prefer or "establish" the groups protected. "Rather," the court said, "it simply avoids penalizing economically the person who conscientiously observes a Sabbath other than Sunday." [33] An appeal to the United States Supreme Court was dismissed last December, the Court holding that the objection did not even raise a substantial federal question.[34] Justice Douglas dissented from the decision, but only on the basis of his general opposition to Sunday laws; in his opinion the Kentucky statute was invalid not because of the exemption, but notwithstanding the exemption.

Problems of religious exemptions (not only from Sunday laws but also from military service and other obligations) require one to consider more closely the nature of the neutrality principle. All exemptions worded in religious terms violate the type of neutrality principle which Professor Philip Kurland has defended in a recent book, *Religion and the Law*,[35] which presents a detailed analysis of all of the Supreme Court cases on church-state relations. He suggests that the "no establishment" and "free exercise" clauses of the First Amendment should not be construed separately but "should be read as a single precept that government cannot utilize religion as a standard for action or inaction because these clauses prohibit classification in terms of religion either to confer a benefit or to impose a burden." [36] Under this principle, any exemption would be invalid if worded in specifically religious terms.

Professor Kurland recognizes that the cases do not follow this line. In the World War I *Selective Draft Law Cases*, the Court brushed off as obviously unsound the contention that exemption of conscientious objectors was invalid because limited to members of particular religious sects whose tenets deny the moral right to engage in war.[37] Professor Kurland is scornful of this decision.[38] In my view, however, such cases are correct. The neutrality principle should not be interpreted as forbidding all specifically religious exemptions. In this respect, the Kurland principle seems to me too formal. The draft law and Sunday law exemptions reflect efforts to protect religious freedom in areas where it would otherwise be limited, in practical effect, by the government's exertion of admitted power. The exemptions are not efforts to promote or establish religion, but merely to maintain neutrality—to see that the action of the government does not operate with hostility to religion.

It is true, of course, that the problem could be avoided by broadening the exemptions. Everyone could be given an option of closing on either Saturday or Sunday. Draft laws could exempt all conscientious objectors, notwithstanding the fact that this would create a difficult administrative task in weeding out pretenders. But I submit that legislatures should not be limited to exemptions of such breadth. In their efforts to avoid restraining religious freedom and to maintain neutrality, legislatures are entitled to discretion in selecting among measures reasonably calculated to achieve their ends.

The principle supporting these exemptions has already been referred to in connection with provisions for religion in the armed forces. Here again, as in our prisons and state hospitals, the purpose of provisions for worship and pastoral care is not to promote religion, but to avoid limiting religious freedom. The principle was well expressed by William Gorman in the words, "No help unless no help would be harm." [39]

In speaking here of protecting religious freedom, I am not referring to the area of freedom which is protected by the Constitution from legislative restraint. Here we are concerned with a wider area, in which legislatures may in their discretion expand religious freedom. Cases interpreting the "no establishment" clause are gradually determining the boundaries of this area.

Neutrality not hostile to religion

I have now introduced all of the main themes which I shall be developing in this series. Let me add some comments on the two contrasting objections to the principle of full neutrality. First I will take up the objection that neutrality is hostile to the American religious tradition.

Under the neutrality principle, the state is in one sense a secular state—but a secular state which does not give preference to secularism and is actively concerned for religious freedom. Recognition of the fact that a secular view of the state is not hostile to religion is now often found in writings coming from widely differing religious traditions. Professor John E. Coons has referred me to a brilliant exposition of this theme by two French Catholic laymen, professors in French universities. They use the term "laical" for the proper secular character of the state.

> This ideal laicity can be called neutrality inasmuch as it denies itself the decision concerning the form which the act of religious liberty will take. . . . But it is not the neutrality of someone who is unaware of religion or who scorns it. On the contrary, the lay state is conscious of being entirely at the service of the liberty of the human spirit; it considers the nation . . . as essentially the milieu where the development of the spirit and the exercise of liberty is made possible.[40]

The article from which I have just quoted is a moving plea to Roman Catholics to re-examine traditional views of the proper state attitude toward religion. The issue of religious freedom which it raises is on the agenda of the Vatican Council, and we shall be considering it further in the third lecture.

In 1892 Justice Brewer wrote for the Court that "this is a Christian nation," [41] and sixty years later Justice Douglas said: "We are a religious people whose institutions presuppose a Supreme Being." [42] But to say this is not to say that our legal institutions may align the state against the secular humanist. In the words of the editor of *The Living Church*, "We are a religious people, expressing our religion through deeply rooted institutions which are not governmental and not subject to popular votes of cities or states." [43]

For the believer, the source of man's responsible freedom is the will of God, and historically the development of Western free institutions is associated with that belief. The secular humanist, however, claims other roots for this freedom and these institutions. He is entitled to neutrality—not merely toleration—so far as our laws are concerned.

But the secular character of the state need not be enforced with rigid absolutism. It is not surprising that the historic religious roots of our institutions are expressed in traditional civic ceremonies and literature and symbols. It is pure pedantry to demand their complete elimination. If this means that our neutrality is a bit more neutral toward some than toward others, a sense of humor should enable all of us to accept the situation and live with our evolving national heritage. I believe that a nativity crèche has no place on the grounds of the Wisconsin State Capitol—but last December I declined to share the initiative in demanding its removal. The subject of the next lecture, religion and public education, provides a test of the acceptability of the neutrality principle and of the point at which violations may be ignored under the *de minimis* principle.

Strict separation

Let me turn to the alternative attack upon the neutrality principle, the attack which asserts that advocates of neutrality are not suspicious enough of organized religion, and that only strict separation will adequately protect the liberties of citizens.

In the *Everson* school bus case, where the majority of the Court applied the neutrality principle, Mr. Justice Jackson was one of the four dissenters. He charged that the majority opinion had undertones inconsistent with the decision itself, undertones "advocating complete and uncompromising separation of Church from State." [44] Indeed, there were such undertones—and more than undertones, for the opinion said at one point, "In the words of Jefferson, the clause against establishment of religion by law was intended to

erect 'a wall of separation between Church and State,' "
(citing the Mormon polygamy case in which Jefferson's
metaphor had been used by the Court for the first time).[45]
Justice Jackson declared that the First Amendment "was intended not only to keep the state's hands out of religion, but
to keep religion's hands off the state, and above all, to keep
bitter religious controversy out of public life by denying to
every denomination any advantage from getting control of
public policy or the public purse." [46]

This theme was amplified in the opinion of Justice Rutledge, in which all four dissenters joined. Paraphrasing
Madison's *Memorial and Remonstrance*, Justice Rutledge
said:

> There cannot be freedom of religion, safeguarded by the
> state, and intervention by the church or its agencies in the
> state's domain or dependency on its largesse. . . . The
> great condition of religious liberty is that it be maintained
> free from sustenance, as also free from other interferences,
> by the state. For when it comes to rest upon that secular
> foundation it vanishes with the resting. . . . Public
> money devoted to payment of religious costs, educational
> or other, brings the quest for more. It brings too the strug-
> gle of sect against sect for the larger share or for any. Here
> one by numbers alone will benefit most, there another. . . .
> The dominating group will achieve the dominant benefit;
> or all will embroil the state in their dissensions.[47]

Chief Justice Warren struck the same note in the Sunday
closing case, explaining that Madison had feared establish-

ment not only because of its threat to religious liberty, but also "because of its tendencies to political tyranny and subversion of civil authority." [48] When Madison was making this argument in the 1780's, he could point to the fact that few of the established clergy had been enthusiastic defenders of the liberties of the colonists. Madison saw in the multiple establishment proposal a rear-guard action by Anglican clergy hoping to preserve their tithes with the help of some of the other Protestant groups. His victory was decisive and of highest importance. Multiple establishment had many of the same dangers as a single established sect. It would clearly violate the "no establishment" clause. It would violate neutrality, throwing the force of the state behind organized religion.

But Madison's plea was for separation, not neutrality. And he was ready to carry the separation principle very far. When President, he vetoed as unconstitutional an act of Congress incorporating a church in the District of Columbia.[49] This policy against incorporation of churches was written into the Virginia constitution, where it remains to this day.[50] But federal statutes have often incorporated religious groups, and the District of Columbia Code, like the laws of most states, makes general provision for such incorporation.[51] The neutrality principle would of course permit the inclusion of religious groups with the other nonprofit organizations which are given the benefits of incorporation.

In many other areas, too, as we have seen, strict separation has never been enforced—and its enforcement would be at an unacceptable cost in terms of religious liberty. This is true in the armed forces, in prisons, and in situations where children are taken over as wards of the state. The District of Columbia Code prescribes that inmates of public institutions shall be given fullest opportunity to practice their religion. Its general rule for foster home placement is that the religion of the foster parents shall be the same as that of the parents.[52] In all these areas, the maintenance of religious freedom has been deemed more desirable than a strict insulation of the state from religious concerns.[53]

Furthermore, where the government enters areas of traditional private and religious activity, such as the building and maintenance of hospitals, a trend toward government monopoly of the field is likely to develop as rising taxes make more difficult the financing of private charities. It is on this ground that one may defend federal grants or loans for hospitals conducted by religious groups as well as other private agencies. It represents an effort to maintain neutrality in a field of expanding government action.

As government activity is extended, instances multiply where strict separation would limit religious freedom and where action which might appear as government aid may be only the result of an effort to maintain full neutrality. A recent instance was furnished by the urban renewal project for the Lincoln Square area in New York. In the plan two blocks were set aside for educational purposes, and Fordham University was permitted to acquire this property from the city. Objections that this constituted aid to sectarian education were overruled. Justice McGivern said, "To hold, under the instant circumstances, that a denominational school may not be afforded the same opportunity to contract as any other private institution or corporation, would be to convert the constitutional safeguards into a sword against the freedoms which they were intended to shield." [54] The Court of Appeals affirmed, saying, "Perhaps this is only another way of saying that, since this sale is an exchange of considerations and not a gift or subsidy, no 'aid to religion' is involved and a religious corporation cannot be excluded from bidding." [55] The United States Supreme Court refused to review this decision, Justice Douglas dissenting.[56] The Court had noted in a previous decision the inclusion of churches in a Washington, D. C. redevelopment project.[57]

The conflict of freedoms

Perhaps a word should be added in defense of the title of this lecture: *Religion and the Conflict of Freedoms*. I have dealt with conflicting freedoms for secular humanists and believers in God. I have brought into the picture the general civil liberties, whose maintenance—in Justice Rutledge's candid language—may require that a price be exacted for the exercise of religious freedom. We have noted the conflict between an established culture-religion and freedom for prophetic criticism. Problems of education are presenting these conflicts in acute form. In the next lecture I shall consider the public school, remembering Justice Frankfurter's dictum that "The non-sectarian or secular public school was the means of reconciling freedom in general with religious freedom." [58]

Finally, it should be said that if all these freedoms were properly defined, perhaps they would not be in conflict. Perhaps conflict arises only because it is forgotten that religious freedom, like other freedoms, is responsible freedom, and that each of us has a religious stake in the religious freedom of others. I shall try to indicate in the final lecture how important are emerging views of the theological basis of religious freedom. Wide support for legislation extending religious freedom can be expected only when citizens are convinced that the groups which ask for freedom can be trusted to respect the religious freedom of all.

After this lecture I was asked whether I fully accept the notion that the Fourteenth Amendment "incorporates" the establishment clause of the First. I answered, "No, but the matter isn't worth fighting over." Let me explain briefly.

Justice Black, among others, has contended that the Fourteenth Amendment incorporates the first nine amendments in their entirety, but this contention has never had majority acceptance. The prevailing view is that the Bill of Rights is imposed on the states only to the extent of the essentials of a system of ordered liberty. If the "no establishment" clause were actually given a strict separation interpretation, I would join those who question the incorporation of this clause by the Fourteenth Amendment. For example, if "no establishment" meant that Congress might not constitutionally provide for incorporation of churches, I would strongly object to extending such a restriction to the states by interpretation of the due process clause. But, as we have seen, neutrality rather than strict separation has usually been the First Amendment canon of interpretation, and neutrality should be required of both state and federal governments, whether by interpretation of the concept of religious liberty or by application of the establishment clause.

I I

Public Education—The Establishment of American Religion?

In 1951 the New York Board of Regents sought "ways to pass on America's Moral and Spiritual Heritage . . . through the public school system." The need was called "dire" because of the "concentrated attacks by an atheistic way of life upon our world" and because of "rising juvenile delinquency." To meet this need, the Board adopted a Statement on Moral and Spiritual Training, part of the strategy of which was to inculcate in school children a "belief in a Supreme Being." To this end, a form of prayer was approved and local authorities were authorized to require its use in public schools. The Regents' prayer was as follows: "Almighty God, we acknowledge our dependence upon Thee, and we beg Thy blessings upon us, our parents, our teachers and our country." [1]

The Board was confident that all "men and women of good will" would subscribe to its program. But in order to avoid infringing the rights of those who might choose to exclude themselves from this category, the Board made provision for voluntary abstention from the use of the prayer.

Eleven years later, the United States Supreme Court found it necessary to decide whether the action of a local board of education prescribing the use of this prayer violated the First Amendment's prohibition of "laws respecting an establishment of religion, or prohibiting the free exercise thereof." While this amendment was originally directed only against Congress, in recent decades it has come to be regarded as applicable also to state legislation by virtue of the Fourteenth Amendment's due process clause.

The Court ruled that the action of the Board of Education was "wholly inconsistent with the Establishment Clause."

> . . . New York's state prayer program officially establishes the beliefs embodied in the Regents' prayer. . . . Neither the fact that the prayer may be denominationally neutral nor the fact that its observance . . . is voluntary can serve to free it from the limitations of the Establishment Clause, as it might from the Free Exercise Clause, of the First Amendment. . . .[2]

The Court denied that its action indicated any hostility to religion and added in a footnote:

There is of course nothing in the decision reached here that is inconsistent with the fact that school children and others are officially encouraged to express love for our country by reciting historical documents such as the Declaration of Independence which contain references to the Deity or by singing officially espoused anthems which include the composer's professions of faith in a Supreme Being, or with the fact that there are many manifestations in our public life of belief in God. Such patriotic or ceremonial occasions bear no true resemblance to the unquestioned religious exercise that the State of New York has sponsored in this instance.[3]

Justice Stewart alone dissented, saying that ". . . to deny the wish of these school children to join in reciting this prayer is to deny them the opportunity of sharing in the spiritual heritage of our Nation." [4]

Lockout of God?

This decision was greeted with a storm of attack. Bishop Pike, for example, declared that the Supreme Court had "deconsecrated the Nation," and that it had achieved a " 'lockout' of God." [5] He listed three possible government policies toward religion: at one extreme, the establishment of a particular church; at the other extreme, the secularization of public life, a policy which he warned had been chosen by Soviet Russia. The third policy he called the middle way, the American experiment, the "public recognition," to quote his language, "by solemn declaration and by prayer—of God and His Providence." But now, he said, "By the [Supreme Court's] opinion 'the middle way' is . . . out, and we are left in logic with the same approach as that of the Communist countries." Bishop Pike called for a constitutional amendment to restore the original meaning of the First Amendment. He believes that the phrase "establishment of religion" clearly refers only to establishing a particular church, an interpretation which I think is untenable for reasons I explained in the first lecture.

The attack on the Supreme Court was as widespread as it was violent. Cardinal Spellman announced that he was "shocked and frightened" by the decision, which "strikes at the very heart of the Godly tradition in which America's children have for so long been raised." [6]

The American Tradition?

A Madison newspaper, the *Wisconsin State Journal*, declared that "The Supreme Court . . . has managed to affront the American tradition and the national heritage with one nit-picking decision, and things are likely to get worse before they can get better." [7] One would not realize from this editorial, or from the hysterical letters from local readers, that over sixty years ago the Wisconsin Supreme Court had unanimously made a similar decision under the state constitution, and that there has been no movement for a corrective amendment.[8] In this case the court forbade regular reading of the King James Bible in public schools. The case arose in the City of Edgerton, and the successful objectors were members of the "very small" Roman Catholic minority. In writing their opinions, two of the three justices apparently agreed to deal respectively with different provisions of the state constitution. Justice Lyons discussed and sustained the objection that the reading of the Bible violated the prohibition of "sectarian instruction" in the common schools. He considered any book sectarian which contains doctrines not accepted by all sects (including Jews). Justice Cassoday discussed and sustained the objection that devotional Bible reading is worship and that the objectors were therefore being forced to support a place of worship. He also indicated that Bible reading falls within the prohibition of "preferring certain religious establishments or modes of worship." In this connection, he quoted with approval a comment of Justice Story on the similar Pennsylvania constitutional provision that "it must have been intended *to extend equally to all sects,* whether they believed in Christianity or not, and whether they were Jews or infidels." [9]

Justice Orton concurred in both opinions and said, "As

the state can have nothing to do with religion except to protect every one in the enjoyment of his own, so the common schools can have nothing to do with religion in any respect whatever. They are as completely *secular* as any of the other institutions of the state." "No state constitution ever existed that so completely excludes and precludes the possibility of religious strife in the civil affairs of the state, and yet so fully protects all alike in the enjoyment of their own religion." [10]

To these quotations, however, must be added the statement of Justice Lyon, that "to teach the existence of a Supreme Being, of infinite wisdom, power, and goodness, and that it is the highest duty of all men to adore, obey, and love Him, is not sectarian, because all religious sects so believe and teach." [11] I find it difficult, to say the least, to reconcile this dictum with Justice Cassoday's reference to equality for infidels or with Justice Orton's emphatic characterization of the common schools as secular.

To return to the Regents' prayer case, there is much controversy, of course, as to the scope of the Supreme Court's ruling. On the facts, the actual decision could deal only with the particular state-composed prayer, and Justice Black's opinion had some emphasis upon this feature, referring to the unfortunate control of the British Parliament over the content of the Anglican Book of Common Prayer. As we all know, the Court now has under advisement cases from other states involving the use of the Lord's Prayer and daily Bible reading. Counsel defending these practices found them clearly distinguishable from the use of the Regents' prayer. It may be rash ever to prophesy concerning the Supreme Court, but I venture rashly to predict that the Court will forbid the use of the Lord's Prayer and also the Bible reading (though here there is more room for doubt since the Court might be tempted to ignore the devotional aspect of the practice).

Neutrality and the public schools

The outlawing of prayer and devotional reading in the public schools can be understood as based on the principle of state neutrality toward religion, the principle which I explained in the first lecture and for which I expressed strong preference. This principle requires the state to be neutral not only between competing religious sects but also between believers and nonbelievers. It means that the influence of the state is not to be thrown either against or in favor of secular humanism. This does not mean that the state must ignore religion. The constitution does not require, as the Court has said, "a callous indifference to religious groups. That would be preferring those who believe in no religion over those who do believe." [12] We saw that in many areas of state activity—for example, in prisons and in the armed forces—affirmative provision for religion may be made—and should be made—if the state is to maintain neutrality and avoid hostility to religion.

Is the neutrality principle desirable in its application to public education, and is neutrality practically feasible in this area? Let me sketch very briefly what neutrality would require and then consider principal alternatives to the neutrality principle.

In public education, neutrality would mean that it is not a function of state schools to inculcate religious beliefs or habits of worship, and that this is true no matter how useful the authorities may regard such beliefs and habits as a basis for the moral values and habits necessary for democratic society. Neutrality would not mean, however, that all references to religion must be rigorously excluded from public school programs. Indeed, rigorous exclusion of the subject of religion from a program of general education would not be neutral; such exclusion would teach by implication the unimportance of religion. In varying ways at the various age levels objective teaching *about* religious beliefs and practices as part of our culture and history may, and indeed should, be included. To say this is not to ignore the difficulty of such objective teaching, particularly in the elementary schools, and particularly in view of the sensitivities of the various groups. I shall be referring later to this problem of feasibility.

We saw in Lecture I that the neutrality principle has been

under recurrent attack from opposite directions. It is attacked by those like Bishop Pike who would permit the state to throw some kinds of support behind religion in general. On the other hand, neutrality is attacked by those who view it as insufficient protection against state involvement in religious strife and who insist upon strict separation. Before considering further the attention which the neutrality principle permits to be given to religion in public education, let us examine some of the recommendations and arguments of the first group of critics.

Tolerance of majority traditions

One of the angry young men who has attacked the Regents' prayer decision is Dean Erwin Griswold of Harvard Law School. He labeled Justice Black's use of the full neutrality principle a "fundamentalist theological approach" savoring of "absolutism." [13] Griswold's principle is that of tolerance. Religious and nonreligious minorities should be tolerated—even welcomed and not disqualified from running for office—but religious toleration should not mean "religious sterility." The Christian majority should be able to express and maintain its religious tradition in public institutions, including public schools. What it means to be a member of a religious minority is to be different in beliefs. "Is it not desirable, and educational," asks the Dean, for the member of a minority "to learn and observe this in the atmosphere of the school—not so much that he is different, as that other children are different from him? . . . No compulsion is put upon him. He need not participate. But he, too, has the opportunity to be tolerant," allowing the majority "to follow their own tradition, perhaps coming to understand and to respect what they feel is significant to them. . . . Learning tolerance may be an important part of American education, and wholly consistent with the First Amendment." "I hazard the thought," Griswold concluded, "that no one would think otherwise were it not for parents who take an absolutist approach to the problem, perhaps encouraged by the absolutist expressions of Justices of the Supreme Court, on and off the bench." [14]

This vigorous expression suggests a number of questions. Is it naive or "fundamentalist" to believe that the American Constitution offers to minorities—or at least attempts to offer them—not tolerance, but equal freedom? What would Griswold say about communities with an overwhelming Roman Catholic majority? Elected school boards in such communities have sometimes expressed the majority tradition by operating the public school virtually as a tax-supported parochial school. I wonder whether Dean Griswold would find this an appropriate lesson in tolerance to be presented to a Protestant minority. We are told that there are communities in the State of Hawaii where the substantial majority is Buddhist. Perhaps Dean Griswold would set limits to the preferential expression of majority religious traditions in public schools. Perhaps the majority whose rights he is anxious to defend must be a generalized Protestant or Christian majority and not some "sect," either Christian or non-Christian.

In any event, however, I had not thought that the First Amendment embodies merely a principle of toleration. Professor Howe has said that leaders in the formative period of our state and national governments aimed at "converting the liberal principle of tolerance into the radical principle of liberty" and "believed that it might be achieved by prohibiting the governmental establishment of religion and guaranteeing religious freedom to all persons." [15]

Establishing an American religion

Other critics of the Regents' prayer decision would permit official recognition not of Christianity as the majority religion, but only of a generalized Judeo-Christian tradition, the Protestant-Catholic-Jewish religion described as an aspect of American culture in Will Herberg's famous book.[16] This seems, indeed, to have been the theory followed by the draftsmen of the Regents' prayer. Under such a policy it appears at first glance that objection might be raised only by adherents of religions outside the Judeo-Christian tradition, by members of Ethical Culture and secular Humanist Societies, and by individualists who disclaim any religious or philosophical affiliation. But this is not the case. Public school support of a general religious tradition is opposed by many Christian and Jewish leaders. The debate is an old one, going back to Horace Mann's proposal for teaching a "common core" of American religion. But, as warned by the American Council on Education, "The notion of a common core suggests a watering down of the several faiths to the point where common essentials appear. This might easily lead to a new sect—a public school sect—which would take its place alongside the existing faiths and compete with them." [17]

Many religious leaders are concerned lest public support establish or entrench the deficiencies of American culture-religion. As they see it, such "religion" is merely a vague religiosity, a religious atmosphere thrown around the American Way of Life. Its effect might be that of a spiritual sedative or an inoculation against all germs of prophetic religion which seeks to judge and reform contemporary culture.

I referred in the first lecture to Peter Berger's book, which has the subtitle *Christian Commitment and the Religious Establishment in America*. The title, *The Noise of Solemn Assemblies*, echoes the prophecy of Amos: "I hate, I despise your feasts, and I take no delight in your solemn assemblies." Berger's theme is that if American religion is to get beyond superficial, dilute religiosity and come to grips with contemporary problems of individual and social life, what is needed is disestablishment—not more, but less recognition and support by the state and its institutions.

Particularly disturbing is the frequency with which the Supreme Court's action is viewed as promoting Communist atheism. I have already quoted Bishop Pike's statement that the Court has left us with no approach but that of the Communist countries. Bishop Pike has not been one of those who identify Christianity with economic conservatism or with chauvinist nationalism, and I had not expected him to provide ammunition for those who believe that secular humanists should be treated as dangerous subversives.

De minimis—or resist beginnings

I have referred to the necessity of avoiding pedantic absolutism in applying the neutrality principle. This certainly applies to public school ceremonies, songs, etc., in which religious notes are sometimes struck. It should apply also to occasional personal expressions of religious belief by teachers or students as individuals. As Professor Paul Freund said from the television screen two weeks ago, there is a conflict between the warning to resist beginnings and the maxim *de minimis non curat lex*. I do not believe that all minor religious observances in public schools need be resisted, but only those which clearly have the shape of an entering wedge. Indeed, I might not have criticized the Supreme Court had they left to the supporters of religion the job of repealing the Regents' prayer.

Neutral concern for religion

We have been considering points on which one group of opponents of the neutrality principle demand a more positive attitude toward religion than neutrality permits. We turn now to the other side of neutrality—the recognition of religion and the active concern for its freedom which neutrality permits (and indeed requires) and which its other group of opponents would forbid.

Neutrality toward religion does not require public authorities to be blind to the facts of religious differences. It does not forbid rules excusing adherents of particular faiths from school attendance on designated religious holidays. This is a point at which the principle suggested by Professor Philip Kurland is too rigid. He has suggested that any

4 6

regulation which uses religion as a basis of classification is contrary to the First Amendment. I trust that he would agree that an exception is appropriate in this case. Attendance excuses, like the exemptions which I discussed in the first lecture, are permissible, not in order to promote religion but to protect its free exercise and thus maintain neutrality.

The same considerations justify regulations adjusting schedules of school extracurricular activities to minimize conflicts with programs of church groups. They apply also to the type of "dismissed time" programs of religious education in which all students are dismissed earlier than usual on certain days to permit voluntary attendance at classes in religion in the various churches and synagogues. Here there can be no claim that the school authorities are exerting pressure in favor of religious education. Extreme separationists, however, might object even at this point, because of a desire to protect school authorities from all such requests or because of concern over supposed "divisive" consequences of any recognition of religious differences.

Released time

There is more serious objection, of course, to programs of "released time" religious education, in which pupils who choose to attend religious classes are excused from school and others are kept in study halls or extra classes. Some degree of influence (not to say coercion) in favor of sectarian education seems unavoidable in such programs, whether the religious classes are held in the public school buildings or in the various churches. The Supreme Court, however, has made the location of the classes the critical fact. The *McCollum* case [18] invalidated the Champaign, Illinois, program, and the *Zorach* case [19] sustained the New York program, which was almost identical except as to location of the classes. There may possibly be a basis for arguing that if the classes are held in the school buildings there is a more direct promoting of their attendance. Then, too, the use of the public building may be considered a financial support of some significance. I agree, however, with the justices who rejected this narrow distinction and therefore dissented in one case or the other.

The broader question is admittedly difficult for an advocate of the principle of neutrality. As the *Yale Law Journal* put it, one must balance the degree of aid to religion which is involved against the degree of limitation of the free exercise of religion which would result if the programs were invalidated.[20] The editor's conclusion was against all released time programs. He would apparently give little weight to the plea of parents who do not favor separate religious schools and yet believe that traditional Sunday School programs leave the impression that religion is a week-end extra, and that exclusion of religion from regular weekday school hours inevitably makes it appear that religion is relatively unimportant and unrelated to daily life.

One of the most penetrating discussions of the released time problem was presented by Alexander Meiklejohn.[21] He disclosed that his personal beliefs were "definitely on the side of nonreligion," and he expressed his skepticism as to the effectiveness of released time programs. But he insisted that it is important in a democratic state that citizens find nourishing roots for belief in democratic values and in the possibility of men's growth in responsible freedom. He noted that for "40 or 50 or 60" per cent of our people religious belief is the source from which democratic institutions derive their moral validity. He noted, too, that "nonbelievers, staggering under the task of finding, within human inspiration itself, an adequate basis for our mode of life, have won, as yet, no secure forms of cooperation or, even, of mutual understanding." [22] "When men are trying to be self-governing," he said, "no other single factor of their experience is more important to them than the freedom of their religion or their nonreligion." [23] He argued that the Constitution requires that religious beliefs shall be given not only equal status but positive status in the public planning of education. And he concluded that such planning might legitimately include released time.

Though much impressed with this argument, I wrote a decade ago that released time programs are consistent with neutrality only if we can assume that programs where students are unconditionally dismissed would be no less successful.[24] And this is a fact which Justice Jackson, for one, was willing to deny categorically. He spoke of the school as serving as a "temporary jail for a pupil who will not go to Church." [25] Perhaps this characterization is open to question; but the *Zorach* case seems clearly wrong in having refused to permit the plaintiffs to prove the coercive operation of the program.

Teaching about religion

Neutrality does not require the elimination from public education of all teaching about religion and religious differences. Indeed, complete elimination of such teaching would violate neutrality. This is particularly true of a school program which attempts to teach moral values. To teach moral values without teaching that many believe these values to have religious roots is to predispose students toward secular humanism. This is a serious problem, for recent studies of public education have reported a more or less deliberate avoidance of religious subject matter, even when it is clearly intrinsic to the discipline concerned.

To the extent feasible, public (as well as private) education should present objective information as to principal religious and nonreligious beliefs. I have emphasized "to the extent feasible" because this presentation of religion is obviously difficult at the elementary school level. Educators tell us, however, that it is not impossible—at least if its legitimacy is recognized and if teachers and school boards are protected from unfair attacks by sectarian and secularist extremists.

But in any event, inclusion of teaching about religion must not mean taking sides against humanist beliefs. Neutrality requires rejecting the demand expressed by a report of a committee of the International Council of Religious Education that the public school should teach the "common religious tradition as the only adequate basis for the life of the school and the personal lives of teachers, students, citizens in a free and responsible democracy." [26]

Rejection of this demand, however, does not mean that the school may not teach the historical evidences of the religious roots of our tradition, evidences such as the references to God in our state constitutions and the Congressionally-approved national motto. Recognition that these religious roots are still very much alive is not inconsistent with a policy of neutrality. But religious teaching is not neutral if it carries any implication that America merely tolerates men like Alexander Meiklejohn and Max Otto, or like John Dewey and Harry Elmer Barnes and the other signers of the 1933 Humanist Manifesto.

I am expressing confident belief that the First Amendment does not forbid objective teaching about religious beliefs in public schools so long as there is no purpose to inculcate such beliefs. And I rather confidently hope that this point will be made clear when the Court decides the cases now pending. But what of state constitution provisions, like that of Wisconsin, forbidding "sectarian instruction" in public schools and in the state university? Do these provisions prescribe not neutrality toward religion but strict separation, an insulation of these public institutions from religion? Do they reflect a determination to keep religious controversy out of these schools even at the cost of inculcating secular humanism? I cannot believe that the answer is yes.

At the University of Wisconsin it should be as possible to have a Department of Religion as it is at Columbia University. Prohibition of "sectarian instruction" should no more prohibit objective study of particular theologies than the parallel statutory prohibition of partisan political instruction forbids teaching about the programs of Republican or Democratic or Communist parties. The problem is one of the purpose and character of the teaching. In the words of Professor A. Campbell Garnett, ". . . the function of the college teaching of religion is not to propagate faith but to enlighten it where it exists and to create an understanding of the faith of others in those who have none of their own, or who have a different faith." "Whether a man . . . is religious or not it is important that his attitude to religion should be one of intelligent understanding. And that is why the study of religion at the university level is needed." [27]

Before going back to the elementary schools, let me digress to mention the abortive attack made some years ago on the University of Minnesota for its efforts to coordinate the activities of religious foundations adjacent to the campus.[28] The objector insisted that his objective was not to make the university a godless institution; that he sought only to prevent infiltration of what he called a "wholly controversial concept of God as taught by religious sectarianism." He saw the problem as one of "protecting religion" by preventing "a few powerful sectarian denominations . . . from gaining such a grip on the campus . . ." What he wanted was to promote within the university what he called "religious activities purely secular in nature." What he apparently did not see was that he was asking the State to discard neutrality and throw its weight behind the "religion" of secular humanism.

At the elementary school level the problem of maintaining neutrality is admittedly more difficult, and a court might therefore interpret a state constitutional provision more strictly in that context. Many questions are left unanswered by close study of the three opinions in the Wisconsin Bible reading case to which I have referred. I wish that the court had put its decision solely on the ground that devotional Bible reading is religious worship and therefore improper in a public school. The holding that the Bible is a sectarian book and its use is therefore sectarian instruction suggests that all teaching concerning sectarian beliefs or practices is forbidden. This obviously need not be the interpretation of the phrase "sectarian instruction." Admittedly, however, the danger is great that community controversy may be touched off by any presentation of religion in the elementary schools. But there is a serious dilemma. Unless this risk is faced and the problem dealt with affirmatively, the alternative risk of promoting secularism is great. If all references to religion must be eliminated, a strong argument will be given to those in various Protestant churches who contend that establishing parish day schools is the only effective way to combat secularism.

The policy statement adopted last year by the directors of the American Civil Liberties Union seems to me excellent. While the Union's position has sometimes seemed one of strict church-state separation, one who prefers a neutrality principle can subscribe without reservation to the following paragraphs:

1. The teaching of religion in the public schools is barred by the Constitution.

2. The practice of regular Bible-reading and organized prayers represents a form of indoctrination which should also be barred.

3. The teaching *of* religion should be distinguished from teaching factually *about* religion as, for example, an element of world history or of social sciences. Even in teaching

about religion, the younger the child, the more wary the teacher must be of indoctrination. Certainly, public schools may *explain* the meaning of a religious holiday, as viewed by adherents of the religion of which it is a part, but may not seek to *foster* a religious view in the classroom or otherwise.

Let me close by recurring to the problem of "divisiveness." As already noted, this term is often used in arguments against teaching about religion in public schools or against programs of released time religious instruction. The same objection is being raised against "shared time" arrangements under which parochial school pupils take some of their subjects in public schools.

The fear of "divisiveness," I take it, is a fear that, if religious differences are publicly recognized, the result is to accentuate the divisions and to exacerbate hostilities already existing. This danger is not imaginary and under some social conditions it may be a controlling consideration. At a time when the dominant character of interfaith relations is one of bitterness, resentment, and distrust, wise legislative and administrative policy may require minimizing occasions for friction and recrimination.

But when we are discussing constitutional policy, the question is different. Are we to interpret the First Amendment on the assumption that serious hostility is the norm in interfaith relations and that legislatures and school boards should therefore be enjoined to take note of religion only by staying away from it? The neutrality interpretation which I have been defending is based on the assumption that American religious pluralism is not so charged with hostility that religious issues must be avoided by enforcing a rigid principle of separation. In words attributed to Dr. Henry Sloan Coffin, perhaps "A certain measure of divisiveness in the community is not too high a price to pay for the maintenance of religious convictions." [29]

III

Religious Schools—The Price of Freedom?

In previous lectures I have considered three competing principles for interpreting the American constitutional tradition on church and state. The principle I have supported is that of state neutrality with respect to religion. Some of the opponents of this principle defend affirmative support of religion, and I examined their claims in the context of public school problems.

The neutrality principle is also opposed—from the opposite side—by those who urge a principle of strict separation of church and state. It is this conflict which we must consider in relation to the financial problems facing church-related schools.

Pierce v. Society of Sisters

After World War I, by the unusual procedure of popular initiative, Oregon passed a law requiring all school children to attend public schools. This measure was held unconstitutional in 1925 in *Pierce v. Society of Sisters*.[1] The *Pierce* case has been widely cited as holding that the right to send children to a religious school is part of the "free exercise of religion" protected by the First Amendment, but this was not the ground of the Court's decision. In 1925 it had not yet been established that the First Amendment's religion clauses were made applicable to state legislation by the due process clause of the Fourteenth Amendment.

The *Pierce* opinion covered two cases, one brought by a Roman Catholic teaching order and the other by a military academy. The Court dealt only with the general concept of liberty protected by the due process clause. It held that:

> The fundamental theory of liberty upon which all governments in this Union repose excludes any general power of the State to standardize its children by forcing them to accept instruction from public teachers only. The child is not the mere creature of the State; those who nurture him and direct his destiny have the right, coupled with the high duty, to recognize and prepare him for additional obligations.[2]

The opinion contained no indication that religious liberty would be given any unique protection in relation to the choice of school.

The central question

In this way it was settled that legislatures must respect the freedom of a parent to choose a religious school. But may legislatures avoid discriminating against religious schools when they enact general measures for the support of education? In other words, may legislatures protect parental freedom of choice by relieving against the over-lapping burden of public school taxes and tuition in a religious school? Many of you, I am sure, will immediately object that I am giving the issue a partisan slant when I state the question in this way. But I think Justice Rutledge (who recognized no such legislative power) would not have objected. In the *Everson* parochial school bus case, he declared that religious liberty, like the freedom of which St. Paul wrote, must be bought with a great price. He added: "And for those who exercise it most fully, by insisting upon religious education for their children mixed with secular, by the terms of our Constitution the price is greater than for others." [3] Our task is to examine the constitutional warrant for this pricing of liberty and to ascertain how large is the price imposed. One who undertakes this task quickly learns that there are many sets of variables of which he should take account.

First, does the question of aid arise under the First Amendment prohibition of laws "respecting an establishment of religion" or under a state constitutional provision which refers more specifically to the expenditure of public funds? If it is a question under the First Amendment, one may perhaps assume that the answer is the same whether a federal statute is in question or whether state legislation is being tested under the Fourteenth Amendment —now that that Amendment has been held to incorporate the First Amendment "no establishment" clause.

Second, what is the nature and extent of the aid in question? Is it a "fringe benefit," as free lunches or bus transportation may perhaps be called? Or is it an educational cost, such as textbooks, teachers' salaries, buildings, or laboratory equipment? And can the aid be clearly enough identified as limited to nonreligious purposes?

Third, what level and kind of education are involved? Is it college or postgraduate study on the one hand or elementary or secondary education on the other? Does it involve an ordinary school or a specialized institution such as an industrial school or a nurses' training school?

Fourth, what form does the aid take? Is it a direct grant (or a loan) to the school, or is it given directly to the student or to his parents in the form of a scholarship or a tax credit or tax deduction?

It is obvious that I shall be able to refer to only a few of the possible permutations of these variables. And there is also a variety of theories for defending (or attacking) the aid, theories more or less plausible with varying combinations of the elements I have listed. Is the aid a benefit to the school or only to the student? Is it merely a government purchase of a service from the school or a mere partial cost reimbursement, and therefore not an "aid" to the school? Is it for a public or merely a private purpose?

Nineteenth-century roots

Even at the risk of serious inaccuracy, I must try to sketch in a paragraph or two the origins of the problem. The controversy goes back at least to the 1820's, when various Protestant schools received tax support in some of the states. This practice declined as public education got under way, but early public schools tended to be close copies of the Protestant schools they replaced. In New York, at least, the unsuccessful Roman Catholic skirmishes to remove Protestant sectarianism from the public schools were part of the setting for the Catholic decision to establish separate schools and to press for a share of tax support. By the middle 40's, the parochial school pattern was becoming settled in New York and the public decision to refuse tax support had been made.

Memory of these sharp controversies may have been taken with them by many of the western migrants. First Michigan, in 1837, and then Wisconsin, in 1848, put into their constitutions the words "nor shall any money be drawn from the treasury for the benefit of religious societies, or religious or theological seminaries." Provisions such as these became common in the new states and spread back to many of the eastern states. They were usually associated with provisions to guard against sectarian control of public schools. Controversy in both areas was recurrent and was associated with successive waves of anti-Catholic feeling.

In 1875 General Grant made the matter a national political issue, and in the following year the so-called Blaine Amendment was introduced, providing that no federal or state funds or credit should be used for the support of any school under the control of any religious (or antireligious) organization. The amendment passed the House but failed of the necessary two-thirds vote in the Senate. Similar efforts to amend the federal constitution have often been made without success.

Everson v. Board of Education

Since 1947 all discussion of the use of public funds for religious schools has to begin with the *Everson* case. In this case the Court sustained, five to four, the New Jersey bus fare reimbursement plan. The decision turned on the interpretation of the First Amendment prohibition of laws "respecting an establishment of religion." As I have said, I read Justice Black's majority opinion as based on a neutrality theory. He said that ". . . the First Amendment . . . requires the state to be neutral in its relations with groups of believers and nonbelievers; it does not require the state to be their adversary. State power is no more to be used so as to handicap religions, than it is to favor them." [4] He said also: ". . . we must be careful, in protecting citizens of New Jersey from state-established churches, to be sure that we do not inadvertently prohibit New Jersey from extending its general state law benefits to all its citizens without regard to their religious belief." [5]

The four dissenters joined in Justice Rutledge's long opinion, which is a classic statement of the strict separation position. It drew largely on James Madison's 1785 *Memorial and Remonstrance* against religious assessments, and the Justice appended to his opinion the full text of the *Memorial*. This document was an eloquent argument for complete separation of church and state, an argument that unless all possibility of government support for churches is eliminated, religious liberty and other liberties are insecure.

Justice Jackson also filed a separate dissenting opinion in which he drew attention to portions of the majority opinion which came close to the separation position. He charged the majority with having weakly compromised its principles, twitting that "The case which irresistibly comes to mind as the most fitting precedent is that of Julia who, according to Byron's reports, 'whispering "I will ne'er consent"—consented.' " [6]

I shall presently return to the *Everson* case and the First Amendment hurdle in the path of broad programs of aid to education. As we shall see, it is by no means clear that the "no establishment" clause forbids inclusion of religious schools in general aid programs. The principle of neutrality which I have discussed in the earlier lectures would permit such inclusion. In the campaign of 1960 Kennedy took the position that aid to religious schools is clearly unconstitutional. He had something of a problem. He was confident that the national welfare required his presence in the White House, and he may well have thought that this end would be jeopardized if he admitted the probable constitutionality of aid to parochial schools. It seems not too wild a guess that he thought that giving up the chance of school aid was not too great a sacrifice to ask of Catholics in order that the nation might gain his services as President. The Kennedy administration has stuck to this constitutional interpretation, but, as we shall see, the contrary interpretation has been made by authorities as impeccable as professors of constitutional law at Harvard.

State constitutions

Before considering further the First Amendment question, I wish to discuss a state constitutional provision which
is typical in having a specific prohibition of payments for
the benefit of sectarian schools. The Wisconsin language is
this: ". . . nor shall any money be drawn from the treasury for the benefit of religious societies, or religious or
theological seminaries." The problem of interpreting such
provisions can conveniently be considered in connection
with the decision last June invalidating an amendment to
the Wisconsin school bus law.[7]

The Wisconsin court first decided—quite properly in my
opinion—that the inclusion of parochial school pupils in the
provision for transportation costs was a benefit to the
schools. The payment from tax funds either would eliminate from the school budget a substantial item of expense
or it would make it easier for families to choose a parochial
school. The court dismissed the "welfare of the child"
argument which has been widely urged as a basis for sustaining such legislation. This is an argument that can be
pressed very far. Payments for major educational costs can
as easily be defended in child welfare terms as can fringe
benefits. Full adoption of the child welfare theory would
practically defeat the clear purpose of a constitutional pro-

hibition like that of Wisconsin. Perhaps the theory is more plausible as applied to transportation benefits (and the theory is indeed suggested by portions of the majority opinion in the *Everson* case). But the Wisconsin court (and the great majority of other state courts) seems to me to have properly construed the specific prohibitions before them when they denied that the difficulty can be conjured away by a "child benefit" rationalization.

The Court, however, weakened the force of its decision by invoking the general neutrality principle which Professor Kurland has extracted from the First Amendment, the principle forbidding all classifications in terms of religion, either to confer a benefit or to impose a burden.[8] The Court used this principle to distinguish tax exemptions which are given to religious institutions only as part of a broad class of nonprofit organizations. The Court held that the benefits under the bus law amendment, while formally extended to all private schools, were limited so as in fact to be available only to parochial schools. In effect, therefore, the Court said that the statutory amendment set up a classification in terms of religion.

I have two difficulties with this reasoning. In the first place, if the Kurland principle is deemed applicable, no religious classification should be found since the statute *as amended* provided bus transportation for public and private schools. My second difficulty is more important. The Kurland principle was suggested as an interpretation of the

First Amendment; I question its applicability in the interpretation of more specific provisions like the Wisconsin prohibition.

The Court's reasoning seems to set the stage for approval of measures which would aid both religious and nonreligious schools; for example, a tax credit or refund for private school tuition payments. Such a credit, it seems to me, runs head on into the state constitutional prohibition. For this purpose a tax credit is the same as a payment from the treasury. I do not think the constitutional prohibition means that aids to religious schools are permissible subject only to the condition that similar aids are extended equally to other private schools. Such clauses are not mere neutrality provisions but provisions for church-state separation. They grew out of the sharp controversies to which I have referred and apparently reflect an intention—to borrow the language of Justice Jackson—"to keep religious controversy out of public life by denying to every denomination any advantage of getting control of . . . the public purse." [9]

But what of college scholarship programs, such as those of Illinois and New York, where state funds may be used for tuition at church-related colleges? [10] Professor Brainerd Currie advised the Illinois Higher Education Commission that there is no serious constitutional question. He relied heavily on a series of Illinois cases permitting state payments to sectarian industrial schools for delinquents. [11] Per-

RELIGION AND AMERICAN CONSTITUTIONS

haps college scholarships, like payments to these special schools, can be distinguished as dealing with areas quite different from the area of parochial school controversy which the constitutional provisions were clearly intended to cover. The problem is troublesome in Wisconsin, however, where the key word is "seminary," a word which the court had early defined as referring to schools at all levels. The difficulty is troublesome but not insuperable, for the New Hampshire court, under a provision applying generally to "schools or institutions of any religious sect," had no difficulty in sustaining a broad program of state aid for nursing education.[12]

Everson again

Let us return to the problem of interpreting the more general language of the First Amendment. Does the *Everson* school bus opinion, with its neutrality language, indicate that the majority judges would have approved tuition aid as well as bus fare reimbursement? One sentence in the opinion needs careful reading: "No tax in any amount, large or small, can be levied to support any religious activities or institutions, whatever they may be called, or whatever form they may adopt to teach or practice religion."[13] This sentence is certainly not free from ambiguity. The question is whether the thrust is against *support of religious teaching* or, more broadly, against any *support of institutions* which give such teaching. The latter interpretation is perhaps more easily justified as a matter of grammar.

But is the *Everson* school bus decision itself "good law" today? One of the justices who made up the bare majority, Justice Douglas, went out of his way in his Regents' prayer opinion last June to say that "The *Everson* case seems in retrospect to be out of line with the First Amendment. Its result is appealing, as it allows aid to be given to needy children. Yet by the same token, public funds could be used to satisfy other needs of children in parochial schools —lunches, books, and tuition being obvious examples." [14] He added that in this case it had been Justice Rutledge who had expressed the "durable First Amendment philosophy."

In 1961, however, the Court had dismissed an appeal from the Connecticut decision sustaining a parochial school bus statute.[15] The dismissal was for failure to present "a substantial federal question." None of the five justices appointed since *Everson* joined Justices Frankfurter and Douglas in dissenting from this action.

One must note, however, that at the same term the Court refused to review on *certiorari* a Vermont decision against school aid.[16] The case arose in a town which had no high school of its own and which was paying tuition for its residents in nearby religious high schools as well as in public high schools. There was no prohibition in the state constitution, but the Vermont court held that the First Amendment forbids such payments.[17] If we were to ignore the rule that denials of *certiorari* are not to be interpreted as indicating opinions on the merits, we might perhaps infer that the toleration of bus transportation aid will not be extended to major costs of education.

Perhaps the next school aid statute to reach the Supreme Court will be the recent Rhode Island act providing for free loan of textbooks to parochial school pupils. On this question another Supreme Court decision is relevant. In 1930 the Court unanimously affirmed a Louisiana case upholding provision of free textbooks.[18] The problem was not considered under the "no establishment" clause, but the decision is a square and unanimous holding that the provision of textbooks for students in parish schools serves a public purpose and that therefore the use of public funds for that purpose is consistent with the due process clause.

Current opinion

Among lawyers, the view that the "no establishment" clause clearly forbids aid to religious schools is not limited to spokesmen for the administration and for "separationist" organizations like the American Civil Liberties Union and the American Jewish Congress. This view has often been expressed so dogmatically that Professor Kurland caustically wrote that "Anyone suggesting that the answer . . . is clear one way or the other is either deluded or deluding." [19] My guess is that the "no aid" view is held by a large majority of lawyers—perhaps I should say, rather, by a large majority of non-Catholic lawyers. The strict separation argument on which it is based is familiar, and I shall turn immediately to the reasoning supporting the contrary position.

This position was taken by all three of us from whom Senator Wayne Morse requested opinions for his Education Subcommittee of the Senate Committee on Labor and Public Welfare. It was most interestingly expressed by Professor Mark DeWolfe Howe, who started with the proposition that "there is no constitutional barrier to Federal financing of the educational activities of [nonreligious] private schools which are serving the public interest by providing that kind of instruction which the States prescribe for public schools." [20] He recognized that a grant to any school for the purpose of constructing a chapel would be unconstitutional. He found no barrier to including sectarian schools in general grants for nonreligious purposes, saying, "I am satisfied that a valid line can be drawn between government support of activities that are predominantly of civil concern and those which are predominantly of religious significance."

Howe dealt with two objections to this position. The first is based on the Roman Catholic claims that religion should permeate the entire school program and does so in Catholic schools. Objectors insist that under this view even laboratories are like chapels and slide rules like religious symbols. Howe conceded that "relentless" logic might support this conclusion, but his answer was that this constitutional issue, like most others, comes down to a question of degree. The second objection was that government support of secular portions of a program releases other funds for religious teaching and practices, and that therefore the "innocence" of people like Howe "will permit bookkeepers to circumvent the prohibitions of the First Amendment." He answered, "Perhaps they are right. I suspect, however, that this bookkeeping habit has become something like a constitutional tradition to which we must adjust ourselves."

Professor Arthur E. Sutherland, Jr. and I reached the same conclusion. I think it is fair to say that for all of us the controlling principle is one of neutrality. Religious schools may not be singled out for preferential aid, but they need not be excluded from a program of general aid, notwithstanding the fact that their inclusion results in indirect aid to religious teaching and practice.

Professor Howe reminded the senators that a program of federal aid may be practically immune from judicial review since federal taxpayers are held to have insufficient standing to raise the constitutional question. He urged therefore that the problem be considered in Congress "with the greatest care and deliberation." And, furthermore, he volunteered his opinion that as a matter of policy "it would be a mistake to make provision at the present time for aid to private elementary and secondary schools."

He dismissed as groundless the notion that a federal aid program limited to public schools would be open to constitutional objection. This notion does seem clearly without foundation, notwithstanding suggestions by Dean Robert F. Drinan and others. A neutrality interpretation of the First Amendment, as I understand it, does not leave to legislatures only the narrow channel between Scylla and Charybdis. Neutrality means that the "no establishment" clause does not forbid aid to religious schools; it does not mean that the "free exercise" clause forbids their exclusion. The First Amendment leaves an area where religious freedom may (but need not) be extended, in the discretion of Congress and the state legislatures.

Incidentally, it is interesting that Senator Abraham Ribicoff, who defended the Administration position when he was Secretary of Health, Education and Welfare, later supported the validity both of limited tax credits for private school tuition and of aid for special purposes in areas such as sciences, mathematics, and foreign languages.[21]

The question of policy

When I turn from the area of constitutional law to that of legislative policy, I find questions of great difficulty. Let me outline some of them and indicate why I do not share Professor Howe's opinion that aid to private elementary and secondary schools would be a mistake and why my opinion, though somewhat diffident, is on the other side.

Before I do so, however, I would like to note that recent Protestant discussions of this problem have shown increased appreciation of its difficulty. For example, in the recent statement adopted by the United Presbyterian General Assembly it was said:

> We . . . share with those who maintain these non-public school systems a stake in the quality of the education they provide. . . . Some of these . . . systems, and notably the Roman Catholic, are subject to critical financial problems not dissimilar to those that face our nation's public schools. . . . It, therefore, ill-behooves United Presbyterians to stand by without concern for what happens to the parochial school system of their Roman Catholic brethren.[22]

While the Report recommends continuing refusal of aid in the form of grants, scholarships, or tax credits, it adds significantly:

United Presbyterians seek discussion with Roman Catholics who share a deep concern for maintaining a strong public school system, with a view to finding new and creative solutions to the present public-parochial school dilemma. Although such suggestions as "shared time" and tax support for scientific and technical parts of school curricula have not yet been adequately formulated, let alone evaluated, United Presbyterians and others should not foreclose future discussions. . . .

I start, as already indicated, with a strong slant in favor of carrying out the neutrality policy which the Constitution permits. While the government should not promote religion, it not only may, but should, try to avoid restraining or burdening religious choices. And if groups wish to have parish schools, there seems to me a presumption in favor of so molding government fiscal policies as not to handicap that choice. For me, therefore, the question is whether there are strong enough grounds for disapproving such schools to justify imposing the handicap. The *Harvard Law Review* comment on the *Everson* case was right in saying that the question is "brutally simple." [23] For these editors the question is: Shall we encourage parochial schools? I might prefer to put it: Shall we continue to discourage parochial schools?

Most of my Protestant and Jewish friends answer Yes, because educational segregation is bad and because encouraging religious schools will undermine the public school system. These are sobering arguments, and we all feel their force. Some observers point to Holland, where education is very largely in the hands of the Catholic and Reformed churches and where society, they argue, is undesirably divided on religious lines. I have made no thorough study of the social and educational issues involved and will only suggest that there are some disadvantages, too, in policies which tend to promote conformity and uniformity through a monolithic school system. And as we noted before, it is not yet clear that public education can avoid promoting secularism. The problem is enormous, and I must leave it without claiming to have justified my position that the presumption against burdening free choice in education has not been rebutted.

Shared time

In one aspect of the problem, the issue is that of divisiveness. This issue is being raised in a new setting in connection with "shared time" proposals and experiments. This phrase refers to arrangements under which parochial school students go to a public school for some of their classes and activities. In some cities this has been done for a long time with respect to manual training and household arts. Some Roman Catholics have expressed hope that extension of this practice might contribute substantially to relief of their financial difficulties. "Shared time" is being tried in a number of communities, in science and other fields, and favorable reports are appearing in the press. (The Wisconsin Supreme Court referred to these programs in the recent school bus case and indicated that they present a less serious constitutional problem than the school bus law.)

"Shared time" might be characterized as "released time" reversed and expanded. Released time programs, which we discussed before, are those where public school pupils are released for religious instruction. Like released time, "shared time" is being opposed as divisive and fraught with possibilities of friction between the different groups of students. On the other hand, it is possible that bringing students together for part of their studies reduces the divisive tendencies inherent in school systems which are entirely separate.

Promoting Roman Catholicism

Should aid to parochial schools be denied for fear of promoting Roman Catholicism? In the recent report to the National Lutheran Council by its Committee on Social Trends, one of the considerations urged against aid to religious schools at the elementary and secondary levels is the point that "the practical effect of the availability of tax funds for [these] schools would be the most gigantic step ever taken by the American people as a whole toward the establishment, for at least several generations, of one or two religious groups which have such school systems—even though such aid were theoretically available to all."

More blunt was the argument advanced in the recent controversy over textbook aid in Rhode Island. Canon Shumaker of the Episcopal Cathedral in Providence said in an address to a Diocesan meeting:

> The Roman Catholic Church regards itself as the sole re-pository of Christian truth. . . . No group which claims that . . . all others are in error has any claim on the public treasury for propagating these views. . . . Roman Catholics are free to believe and teach anything they like. But Episcopalians do not have to help them do it.[24]

This argument troubles me. I wonder whether the claims of Rhode Island Episcopalians to Christian truth as they understand it are so different from the claims of responsible Roman Catholics. I cannot believe that Canon Shumaker would agree with Professor Howe's suggestion that skepticism is "an essential element in the spirit of the latter-day Protestant" and that this is why "the well-behaved Episcopalian [or] Presbyterian" is hesitant to pronounce his neighbor's convictions as false.[25] But, in any event, it is not clear that unjustified claims to religious truth make unjust the Roman Catholic claims as to educational budgets. Professor Howe did predict, however, the following:

It is unlikely that the equality which results from liberty will be attained by any church which is committed, or seems to the bulk of the community to be committed, to the doctrine not only that all men are obligated to seek and follow the truth, but that the truth is to be found in its faith only.[26]

Roman Catholic schools

Arguments against nondiscriminatory aid sometimes include frank condemnation of Roman Catholic schools. In 1958 a conference on Religion in a Free Society was sponsored by the Fund for the Republic and was attended by leaders of what Fr. John Courtney Murray referred to as the "four conspiracies"—Catholic, Protestant, Jewish, and secularist.[27] Professor James Hastings Nichols, an authority on church history, said this about parochial schools:

Protestants are concerned . . . [because] Roman Catholic controlled education is censored education, and a part of a general strategy to establish enclaves of concentrated clerical political power, withdrawn from the democratic determination of policy by discussion. To that degree its graduates are crippled as contributors to the great dialogue of our common life. One cannot force a man to enter into a democratic discussion if he does not believe in democracy or discussion, but does "distributive justice" require that we subsidize his secession from the civic dialogue? [28]

I need not tell you that this address "broke the ice" and that later "discussion" was uninhibited. Last year Professor Nichols was one of the Presbyterian observers at the Vatican Council. After his return he spoke at the University of Iowa, giving a dialogue report on the council with Bishop Tracy of the Catholic Diocese of Baton Rouge. Nichols said:

> I hadn't realized that anything like this existed. . . . I thought the Roman Catholic Church was a very closed, complacent and sectarian body that had nothing to learn from anybody else. I now know that this is no longer accurate, if it ever was.[29]

He added:

> I would like to express the certainty that there is here in this church [the Catholic Church] a genuineness of Christian religion and faith that is unmistakable. Even while I am still intellectually baffled to account for many aspects of the theological position of the church, I know that the reality of Christ's church is here.

I wonder whether Professor Nichols has acquired also some hope that Catholic education is not, or need not be, as he had described it.

Catholicism and religious liberty

Another factor which sometimes comes to the surface in these controversies is distrust of the ambiguities in the

Roman Catholic position on religious liberty and church-state relations. An arresting item recently appeared in *Church and State,* the monthly organ of Protestants and Other Americans United, the most militant opponent of parochial school aid. The editors had unearthed a book by Msgr. James T. Booth, who is Chancellor of the Diocese of San Diego, entitled "Church Educational Problems in the State of California." It was published in Rome in 1960. Passages were quoted which included the following:

> The toleration of separation of Church and state can be for a time . . . but the duty of the members of the Church is to continually advance the cause of the Church for complete union of Church and State. So the problem of the leaders of the Church is to obtain as many benefits as possible, and to get as near to a situation of union of Church and State as possible, without revealing in action or demand the ultimate necessity of union. In America, many advantages of the Church would disappear if an out and out statement of desired union were even mentioned.[30]

These words are so shocking that I hesitated to quote them without personal verification. I do so, however, after correspondence with the author, who tells me that copies of the book are not available.[31]

If Msgr. Booth's book represented the official Catholic position, I believe it would fully justify refusal of economic freedom for parochial schools. But this is almost a caricature of the old Catholic view of "ideal" church-state relations, a view which took form long before the development of democratic government. Its applicability in conditions of American democracy has been denied by the American hierarchy. And what is more hopeful, because it is positive, is the fact that Catholic scholars, here and in Europe, have been developing a strong doctrine of religious liberty. Fr. Murray said over a decade ago that ". . . the protection of the religious unity of society, by suppression of error and dissent, is not among the political functions of government." [32] He wrote also:

> . . . in the democratic concept of civil liberty, the idea of religious liberty has the same amplitude as the idea of civil liberty itself. As it declares the civic equality of all citizens before the law, so it likewise declares the civic equality of all churches . . . before the law. As it recognizes equal liberty for the public expression of any political idea, even though it be contrary to the common civic beliefs, so it recognizes equal liberty for the public expression of any religious ideas, . . . [33]

Furthermore, religious freedom is being supported by Catholic scholars on theological grounds. Fr. Henri-Dominique Robert bases religious freedom "not only, or even primarily, on the dignity of man or on the good of civil peace, but *on the claim of God demanding of men His due, that is to say the unconstrained tribute of human freedom.*" This way of looking at things, he says, "is firmly theocentric: the reasons and the finality it confers on the mutual respect of our spiritual divisions are explicitly supernatural and are derived from the demands God Himself makes upon man." [34]

The subject of religious liberty is on the agenda of the Vatican Council, and there seem to be grounds to hope for a vigorous pronouncement. Ten years ago I thought that the ambiguity of the Catholic stand on religious freedom might be sufficient reason for the withholding of equality in programs of aid to education. Today, I am certain that it is not. What is needed today, I think, is an expression of trust that as Catholics and Protestants, Christians and non-Christians, believers and nonbelievers, we are all being led to deeper truth concerning religious freedom.

What such trust should mean by way of immediate recognition of the financial problems of parochial schools, I cannot say. It would certainly mean cordial openness to experiment with programs such as "shared time." Perhaps it may be just as well that many state constitutions keep the massive core of the problem temporarily out of the political arena. Perhaps it is just as well if the problem is first explored as part of the federal government's supplementary aid to education. I do not underestimate the possibility of bitter strife in this area, but I cannot believe that Americans are so unable to face these questions that the present situation of injustice must be maintained forever.

I have been supporting in these lectures a principle of neutrality—not neutrality for its own sake, but neutrality in order that religion may have freedom—and not only external freedom from restraint, but also the interior freedom which is literally essential to the religious act. And that interior freedom can be possessed only as it is affirmed for all men. That is what I meant in the first lecture when I said that each of us has a stake, a religious stake, in the religious freedom of all.

In some times and places the maintenance of religion's external freedom from government restraint may be the most pressing task. But in America today there is at least equal need for protecting the interior freedom of religion from the numbing corruption of government aid.

I am reminded of the difficulty with which the Christian missionary effort learned that potential converts should not be corrupted. The dangers of making "rice Christians" or of using political influence was sometimes discovered too late. In the 1920's the philosopher William E. Hocking took part in an extensive study of missionary strategy. It was after this experience that he wrote:

> . . . religion is never political in its nature. It has no speech except to free spirits. Its aim is to draw men to devotion . . . and a devotion that is enforced is not sincere. . . . When it mistakenly uses the organs of power the very object of religion is undermined.[35]

It is for this reason, in the end, that Justice Black's First Amendment principle "no aid to all religions" should be given thankful approval.

8 6

The government must not aid; but it should be vigilant also lest the exertion of its expanding powers handicap the exercise of religious freedom. Therefore the government may, and should, make affirmative provision for religion in areas such as those we have been considering. This is the policy of neutrality. It can be reflected in our law and practice—and religious freedom can thereby be maximized —but this will come about only if Americans can trust each other's belief that religion must indeed be free.

EPILOGUE

Neutrality as of June 1963

THROUGH THE FOREGOING LECTURES runs the theme that the impact of the First Amendment on religion is best understood in terms not of church-state separation but of government neutrality—neutrality not merely between sects, but also between believers and nonbelievers. This broad neutrality is promoted by judicial action checking legislative aberrations in either direction. But in many fields where laws affect religion incidentally, the promotion of neutrality requires affirmative provision for religion. Here legislatures have been left with discretion; in this area provisions affirmatively fostering religious freedom are not invalid as "establishing" religion, but their omission does not make the legislation invalid as a restraint on "free exercise" of religion.

On June 17, 1963, the Supreme Court expounded the

neutrality principle at length when it construed the "no establishment" clause as forbidding religious practices in public schools.[1] On the same day, the Court restricted the area in which promotion of neutrality is left to legislative discretion. It held that when a state denies unemployment compensation to those not "available" for work, the "free exercise" clause requires an exception for those whose religious convictions make them unavailable for work on Saturdays.[2]

Neutrality and disestablishment

Justice Clark spoke for eight justices in the public school cases which involved recitation of the Lord's Prayer and devotional reading of the Bible. The two cases are reported together as *School District of Abington Township v. Schempp.* The idea of neutrality is referred to repeatedly in all of the five opinions. As Justice Clark put it, the two religion clauses of the First Amendment place the government in a "neutral position." [3] He spoke of "The wholesome 'neutrality' of which this Court's cases speak" [4] and quoted passages using the words "neutral" and "neutrality" from the Black and Jackson opinions in the *Everson* school bus case.[5] Justice Clark warned that "The breach of neutrality that is today a trickling stream may all too soon become a raging torrent." He declared:

. . . we cannot accept that the concept of neutrality, which does not permit a State to require a religious exercise even with the consent of the majority of those affected, collides with the majority's right to free exercise of religion. While the Free Exercise Clause clearly prohibits the use of state action to deny the rights of free exercise to *anyone*, it has never meant that a majority could use the machinery of the State to practice its beliefs.[6]

The emphasis was clearly on neutrality—a policy required lest "powerful sects or groups might bring about a fusion of governmental and religious functions or a concert or dependency of one upon the other . . ."[7] The Court quoted also the Rutledge language in *Everson* that the object of the First Amendment "was to create a complete and permanent separation of the spheres of religious activity and civil authority . . ."[8] and the Frankfurter statement in the *Mc-Collum* released time case that "[s]eparation is a requirement to abstain from fusing functions of government and of religious sects."[9] Also quoted was Justice Douglas' language in the *Zorach* released time case that the amendment "does not say that in every and all respects there shall be a separation of Church and State."[10]

The concurring opinion of Justice Goldberg agreed that "the attitude of the state toward religion must be one of neutrality," adding that the concept of neutrality should not have an "untutored devotion"[11] which could lead to "a brooding and pervasive devotion to the secular." Justice

Harlan joined in this opinion. Justice Brennan's long concurring opinion declared that the "State must be steadfastly neutral in all matters of faith." [12] He noted that "insistence upon neutrality, vital as it surely is for untrammelled religious liberty, may appear to border on religious hostility. But in the long view, the independence of both church and state in their respective spheres will be better served by close adherence to the neutrality principle." [13]

Justice Stewart alone dissented. He, too, accepted a principle of "government neutrality" which requires "extension of even handed treatment to all who believe, doubt, or disbelieve—a refusal on the part of the State to weight the scales of private choice." [14] In his view, however, there is no departure from neutrality without some degree of coercion. He voted to have the cases remanded for further testimony on the coercion issue, urging that certain types of religious exercises would involve no possibility of practical coercion—as where they were scheduled as "merely one among a number of desirable alternatives." [15] He added that if the record showed "that the timing of morning announcements by the school was such as to handicap children who did not want to listen to the Bible reading, or that the excusal provision was so administered as to carry any overtones of social inferiority, then impermissible coercion would clearly exist." [16]

Neutrality in public schools

The Court's test for the application of the neutrality principle is whether the "purpose or primary effect" of an enactment is "either the enhancement or inhibition of religion." "That is to say that to withstand the strictness of the Establishment Clause there must be a secular legislative purpose and a primary effect that neither advances nor inhibits religion." [17] ". . . the fact that individual students may absent themselves upon parental request . . . furnishes no defense to a claim of unconstitutionality under the Establishment Clause." [18]

In the opinion of the majority, the religious practices under attack failed to meet this test. The Court took note of the contention that the elimination of these practices would establish a "religion of secularism."

> We do not agree, however, that this decision in any sense has that effect. In addition, it might well be said that one's education is not complete without a study of comparative religion or the history of religion and its relationship to the advancement of civilization. It certainly may be said that the Bible is worthy of study for its literary and historical qualities. Nothing we have said here indicates that such study of the Bible or of religion, when presented objectively as part of a secular program of education, may not be effected consistent with the First Amendment.[19]

Justice Goldberg added, "it seems clear to me from the opinions in the present and past cases that the Court would recognize the propriety of . . . the teaching *about* religion, as distinguished from the teaching *of* religion, in the public schools." [20]

Justice Brennan said:

> The holding of the Court today plainly does not foreclose teaching *about* the Holy Scriptures or about the differences between religious sects in classes in literature or history. Indeed, whether or not the Bible is involved, it would be impossible to teach meaningfully many subjects in the social sciences or the humanities without some mention of religion. To what extent, and at what points in the curriculum, religious materials should be cited, are matters which the courts ought to entrust very largely to the experienced officials who superintend our Nation's public schools. They are experts in such matters, and we are not. We should heed Mr. Justice Jackson's caveat that any attempt by this Court to announce curricular standards would be "to decree a uniform, rigid and, if we are consistent, an unchanging standard for countless school boards representing and serving highly localized groups which not only differ from each other but which themselves from time to time change attitudes." [21]

Justice Brennan added, "If it should sometime hereafter be shown that in fact religion can play no part in the teaching of a given subject without resurrecting the ghost of the practices we strike down today, it will then be time enough to consider questions we must now defer." [22]

In view of all these careful statements, there seems little warrant for the declaration of the *Wall Street Journal* that the Supreme Court has established atheism as "the one belief to which the State's power will extend its protection," [23] or the statement of Bishop Pike that "The result of the decision is not neutrality but an imposition upon the public school system of a particular perspective on reality, namely, secularism by default, which is as much an 'ism' as any other." [24]

In some states compliance with the Court's decision will apparently await further litigation. It is being said in many quarters that "voluntary" religious devotions are still authorized in public schools. If this means that individual teachers are free to set up regular devotional programs, the contention seems clearly inconsistent with the *Schempp* decision, since the thrust of the opinion is against all use of the authority of the state whether by legislatures, school boards, or teachers. It must be remembered that the programs before the Court were "voluntary" in the sense that children of objecting parents might be excused from participation.

Neutrality and legislative discretion

In the *Schempp* case, only Justice Brennan had occasion to refer to the area of legislative discretion in the promoting of neutrality. He cited provisions for religion in the armed forces, saying the following:

> . . . hostility, not neutrality, would characterize the refusal to provide chaplains and places of worship for prisoners and soldiers cut off by the State from all civilian opportunities for public communion, [or] the withholding of draft exemptions for ministers and conscientious objectors . . . I do not say that government *must* provide chaplains or draft exemptions, or that the courts should intercede if it fails to do so.[25]

The problem of legislative discretion became critical in *Sherbert v. Verner*, the unemployment compensation case decided simultaneously with *Schempp*. Seven justices held that a state might not deny compensation to a Seventh-day Adventist who would not accept a position requiring work on Saturday. Justice Brennan's majority opinion insisted that the decision "reflects nothing more than the governmental obligation of neutrality in the face of religious differences." [26] Justice Harlan wrote in dissent as follows:

> The constitutional obligation of "neutrality" . . . is not so narrow a channel that the slightest deviation from an absolutely straight course leads to condemnation. There are too many instances in which no such course can be charted, too many areas in which the pervasive activities of the State justify some special provision for religion to prevent it from being submerged by an all-embracing secularism.[27]

Presumably, the majority did not disagree with this general statement, but they did deny that the area of legislative discretion included the case before them.

Justice Brennan had been one of the dissenters in *Braunfeld v. Brown*,[28] the decision refusing to require a sabbatarian exemption in Sunday closing laws. He attempted, however, to distinguish the case at bar from *Braunfeld* on two grounds. The burden imposed upon religious practices by Sunday closing laws was said to be "less direct" than that imposed by the disqualification to receive unemployment compensation. Furthermore, the state interests involved in the two cases were said to be "wholly dissimilar," and the problems of competition and administration raised by a closing law exemption were said to have been considered so serious as to threaten the workability of the entire statutory scheme. These grounds of distinction were rejected by the dissenters and also by Justice Stewart, who had voted with Brennan in the Sunday law cases. The first ground seems to me clearly untenable. As to the second, it can perhaps be argued persuasively that only a small burden was placed on non-sabbatarians by way of increased cost of the compensation system resulting from the decision in *Sherbert*, whereas non-sabbatarian merchants might be placed at a substantial competitive disadvantage if exemptions from Sunday closing regulations were granted to sabbatarians.

Stewart's concurring opinion in *Sherbert* is a continuation of his *Schempp* dissent. He charged the Court with trying to "paper over" an inconsistency in requiring under the "free exercise" clause a religious exemption which its "fundamentalist" reading of the "no establishment" clause would logically require it to forbid.

> . . . the guarantee of religious liberty embodied in the Free Exercise Clause affirmatively requires government to create an atmosphere of hospitality and accommodation to individual belief or disbelief. In short, I think our Constitution commands the positive protection by government of religious freedom—not only for a minority, however small—not only for the majority, however large—but for each of us.[29]

In *Schempp* he thought that the record did not show that the school authorities had failed to maintain an atmosphere of hospitality to disbelief. But notwithstanding the strong language just quoted, presumably Justice Stewart would not *require* school authorities to show hospitality to belief by providing devotional exercises.

Hints on public funds for church schools

The opinions of June 17th are being combed for dicta concerning the use of public funds for church-related schools, but the search is disappointing. Of course, it was to be expected that Justice Douglas would take every opportunity to express again his view that the establishment

47523

clause forbids any such expenditures. In the Regents'
Prayer case he had said, "The point for decision is whether
the Government can constitutionally finance a religious
exercise." [30] In *Schempp,* he again approached the problem
as one of financing religion:

> . . . the Establishment Clause . . . forbids the State to em-
> ploy its facilities or funds in a way that gives any church,
> or all churches, greater strength in our society than it
> would have by relying on its members alone. Thus, the
> present regimes must fall under that clause for the addi-
> tional reason that public funds, though small in amount,
> are being used to promote a religious exercise. Through the
> mechanism of the State, all of the people are being required
> to finance a religious exercise that only some of the people
> want and that violates the sensibilities of others.
>
> *The most effective way to establish any institution is to
> finance it; and this truth is reflected in the appeals by
> church groups for public funds to finance their religious
> schools.* Financing a church either in its strictly religious
> activities or in its other activities is equally unconstitu-
> tional, as I understand the Establishment Clause. Budgets
> for one activity may be technically separable from budgets
> for others. But the institution is an inseparable whole, a
> living organism, which is strengthened in proselytizing
> when it is strengthened in any department by contribu-
> tions from other than its own members.[31] [The italics are
> in the opinion.]

In *Sherbert,* Justice Douglas said, "The fact that government cannot exact from me a surrender of one iota of my

religious scruples does not, of course, mean that I can demand of government a sum of money, the better to exercise them. For the Free Exercise Clause is written in terms of what the government cannot do to the individual, not in terms of what the individual can exact from the government." [32]

Justice Brennan, in the concluding section of his *Schempp* opinion, discussed types of "cooperation or accommodation between religion and government" which are permissible notwithstanding the establishment clause. In his opinion these permissible "forms of involvement" show that "the First Amendment commands not official hostility toward religion, but only a strict neutrality in matters of religion." [33] Tax exemption was one of his illustrations:

> Nothing we hold today questions the propriety of certain tax deductions or exemptions which incidentally benefit churches and religious institutions, along with many secular charities and nonprofit organizations. If religious institutions benefit, it is in spite of rather than because of their religious character. For religious institutions simply share benefits which government makes generally available to educational, charitable, and eleemosynary groups. There is no indication that taxing authorities have used such benefits in any way to subsidize worship or foster belief in God. And as among religious beneficiaries, the tax exemption or deduction can be truly nondiscriminatory, available on equal terms to small as well as large religious bodies, to

popular and unpopular sects, and to those organizations which reject as well as those which accept a belief in God.[34]

Justice Brennan gave this paragraph an italicized heading, *"Uniform Tax Exemptions Incidentally Available to Religious Institutions."* One can only speculate whether he would be willing to defend in similar terms "Uniform Provisions for Educational Costs Incidentally Available to Religious Schools."

As already noted, Justice Stewart spoke of neutrality as requiring "a refusal on the part of the State to weight the scales of private choice." [35] Again, one can only speculate as to how he would regard an effort by a state or the federal government to avoid financial weighting of the scales of parental choice between public and parochial schools.

These opinions of June 17, 1963, covered 144 pages. One expert commentator sees in them a groping for doctrine which accomplishes only obfuscation.[36] In my view, the Court has taken an important step in putting primary emphasis on neutrality, a principle which protects religion from government sponsorship as well as government restraint. What remains to be clarified is the extent of legislative discretion in promoting neutrality.

NOTES

I. RELIGION AND THE CONFLICT OF FREEDOMS

1. Wis. Const. art. I, § 18.
2. Wis. Const. art. X, §§ 3, 6.
3. Torcaso v. Watkins, 367 U.S. 488 (1961). The Court had come a long way since 1892 when Mr. Justice Brewer cited similar state constitutional provisions as showing that "this is a religious nation." Church of the Holy Trinity v. United States, 143 U.S. 457, 469–70 (1892).
4. Torcaso v. Watkins, 367 U.S. 488, 495 (1961). The Court also referred to two tax exemption cases: Washington Ethical Society v. District of Columbia, 249 F.2d 127 (D. C. Cir. 1957); Fellowship of Humanity v. County of Alameda, 153 Cal. App. 2d 673, 315 P.2d 394 (1957).
5. See Barnes and Rosenfeld, *Is Humanism a New Religion?* 22 The Humanist 127 (1962); Wilson, *The Religious Element in Humanism, id.* at 173 (1962).
6. Parsons, The First Freedom 79 (1948).

7. 330 U.S. 1, 15–16 (1947).
8. Engel v. Vitale, 370 U.S. 421 (1962).
9. Committee on Judiciary, 87th Cong., 2d Sess., Hrgs. on S.J. Res. 205, July 26, 1963, 51, 55.
10. See Corwin, *The Supreme Court as National School Board*, 14 Law & Contemp. Prob. 3 (1949); Pfeffer, Church, State, and Freedom ch. 5 (1953).
11. Howe, *The Constitutional Question*, in Religion and the Free Society 57 (Fund for the Republic 1958).
12. 1 Annals of Cong. 434 (June 8, 1789) (1834).
13. *Id.* at 731 (August 15, 1789).
14. *Id.* at 766 (August 20, 1789).
15. Journal of the First Session of the United States Senate 116–17 (1820).
16. *Id.* at 128.
17. Van Deusen, *Prayer, Religion and the Nation*, 22 Christianity and Crisis 178 (1962).
18. 28 Journals, Cont. Cong. 293–95 (April 23, 1785). (Lib. of Cong. ed. 1936).
19. Brandt, James Madison, The Nationalist 353 (1948).
20. 33 Journals, Cont. Cong. 400 (Lib. of Cong. ed. 1936).
21. Everson v. Board of Education, 330 U.S. 1, 18 (1947).
22. *Id.* at 16.
23. McGowan v. Maryland, 366 U.S. 420 (1961); Gallagher v. Crown Kosher Super Market, 366 U.S. 617 (1961); Braunfeld v. Brown, 366 U.S. 599 (1961); Two Guys from Harrison-Allentown, Inc. v. McGinley, 366 U.S. 582 (1961); Arlan's Department Store of Louisville, Inc. v. Kentucky, 371 U.S. 218 (1962).
24. Griswold, *Absolute Is in the Dark*, 8 Utah L. Rev. 167, 177–79 (1963).
25. McGowan v. Maryland, 366 U.S. 420, 438 (1961).
26. Braunfeld v. Brown, 366 U.S. 599, 616 (1961).
27. *Id.* at 609.

28. McGowan v. Maryland, 366 U.S. 420, 576 (1961).
29. Relations Between Church and State, A Report to the 174th General Assembly 15 (1962).
30. Shreveport v. Levy, 26 La. Ann. 671, 672 (1874).
31. Braunfeld v. Brown, 366 U.S. 599, 608 (1961).
32. McGowan v. Maryland, 366 U.S. 459, 520 (1961). (Separate opinion filed in both cases.)
33. Commonwealth v. Arlan's Department Store of Louisville, 357 S.W. 2d 708, 710 (Ky. 1962).
34. Arlan's Department Store of Louisville v. Kentucky, 371 U.S. 218 (1962).
35. Kurland, Religion and the Law (1962) (reprint of article, *Of Church and State and the Supreme Court,* 29 U. Chi. L. Rev. 1 (1961)).
36. Kurland, Religion and the Law 18 (1962).
37. Selective Draft Law Cases, 245 U.S. 366, 389–90 (1918).
38. Kurland, Religion and the Law 38 (1962).
39. Gorman, *A Case of Distributive Justice* in Religion and the Schools 34, 60 (Fund for the Republic 1959).
40. Vialatoux and Latreille, *Christianity and Laicity,* 2 Cross-currents 15, 19 (1952). Cf. Munby, The Idea of a Secular Society (1963).
41. Church of the Holy Trinity v. United States, 143 U.S. 457, 471 (1892).
42. Zorach v. Clauson, 343 U.S. 306, 313 (1952).
43. *How to be Religious, Though American,* The Living Church, July 29, 1962, p. 11.
44. Everson v. Board of Education, 330 U.S. 1, 19 (1947).
45. *Id.* at 16.
46. *Id.* at 26–7.
47. *Id.* at 53–4.
48. McGowan v. Maryland, 366 U.S. 420, 430 (1961).
49. The veto message is quoted in full in 3 Stokes, Church and State in the United States 414 (1950).

50. Va. Const., § 59.
51. Dist. Col. Code. § 29–601 (1961).
52. *Id.* § 3–123 (1961).
53. *Ibid.*
54. 64th St. Residences v. City of New York, 173 N.Y.S. 2d 700, 703 (Sup. Ct. 1957).
55. 4 N.Y. 2d 268, 276, 150 N.E. 2d 396, 399 (1958).
56. Harris v. City of New York, 357 U.S. 907 (1958).
57. Berman v. Parker, 348 U.S. 26, 34–5 (1954).
58. McCollum v. Board of Education, 333 U.S. 203, 216 (1948).

II. PUBLIC EDUCATION—THE ESTABLISHMENT OF AMERICAN RELIGION?

1. Quotations in this and the following paragraph are from the Record and Brief of the Board of Regents in Engel v. Vitale, cited in Kurland, *The Regents' Prayer Case: "Full of Sound and Fury, Signifying . . . ,"* [1962] Sup. Ct. Rev. 1, 4–5.
2. Engel v. Vitale, 370 U.S. 421, 424, 430 (1962).
3. *Id.* at 435, n. 21.
4. *Id.* at 445.
5. The Rt. Rev. James A. Pike, Bishop of the Episcopal Diocese of California, Address Before the Commonwealth Club of California, press release July 13, 1962.
6. Religious News Service, New York, June 26, 1962.
7. Wisconsin State Journal, December 7, 1962, sec. 1, p. 6.
8. State ex rel. Weiss v. District Board, 76 Wis. 177, 44 N.W. 967 (1890).
9. Vidal v. Girard's Ex'rs, 2 How. 128, 198 (1844).
10. State ex rel. Weiss v. District Board, 76 Wis. 177, 218, 220, 44 N.W. 967, 981 (1890).
11. *Id.* at 193–94, 44 N.W. at 973.
12. Douglas, J., in Zorach v. Clauson, 343 U.S. 306, 314 (1952).

13. Griswold, *Absolute Is in the Dark*, 8 Utah L. Rev. 167, 172 (1963).
14. *Id*. at 176–7.
15. Howe, review of Stokes, Church and State in the United States, 64 Harv. L. Rev. 170, 171–72 (1950).
16. Herberg, Protestant, Catholic, Jew (1955, 1960).
17. Report of American Council on Education Committee on Religion and Education, The Relation of Religion to Public Education—The Basic Principles 15 (1947).
18. McCollum v. Board of Education, 333 U.S. 203 (1948).
19. Zorach v. Clauson, 343 U.S. 306 (1952).
20. *Released Time Revisited: The New York Plan Is Tested*, 61 Yale L. J. 405 (1952).
21. Meiklejohn, *Educational Cooperation Between Church and State*, 14 Law and Contemp. Prob. 61 (1949).
22. *Id*. at 63.
23. *Id*. at 67.
24. Katz, *Freedom of Religion and State Neutrality*, 20 U. Chi. L. Rev. 426, 439 (1953).
25. Dissenting in Zorach v. Clauson, 343 U.S. 306, 324 (1952).
26. Quoted in Bennett, Christians and the State 240 (1958).
27. Garnett, *Should the University Teach Religion?* Wisconsin Alumnus, December, 1950, p. 15.
28. State ex rel. Sholes v. University of Minnesota, 236 Minn. 452, 54 N.W. 2d 122 (1952), Brief of Appellant.
29. Quoted in address by the Rev. James A. Pike at General Theological Seminary, May 22, 1951.

III. RELIGIOUS SCHOOLS—THE PRICE OF FREEDOM?

1. 268 U.S. 510 (1925).
2. *Id*. at 535.
3. Everson v. Board of Education, 330 U.S. 1, 59 (1947).

4. *Id.* at 18.
5. *Id.* at 16.
6. *Id.* at 19.
7. State ex rel. Reynolds v. Nusbaum, 17 Wis. 2d 148, 115 N.W. 2d 761 (1962).
8. Kurland, Religion and the Law 18, 112 (1962).
9. Everson v. Board of Education, 330 U.S. 1, 27 (1947).
10. Ill. Rev. Stat. ch. 122, art. 30 (1961); N.Y. Education Law, art. 13 (McKinney, 1961).
11. Dunn v. Chicago Industrial School, 280 Ill. 613, 117 N.E. 735 (1917).
12. Opinion of Justices, 99 N.H. 519, 113 A.2d 114 (1955).
13. Everson v. Board of Education, 330 U.S. 1, 16 (1947).
14. Engel v. Vitale, 370 U.S. 421, 443 (1962).
15. Snyder v. Town of Newtown, 365 U.S. 299 (1961).
16. Anderson v. Swart, 366 U.S. 925 (1961).
17. Swart v. South Burlington School Dist., 122 Vt. 177, 167 A.2d 514 (1961).
18. Cochran v. Louisiana State Board of Education, 281 U.S. 370 (1930).
19. Kurland, Religion and the Law 111 (1962).
20. Constitutionality of Federal Aid to Education in its Various Aspects, Sen. Doc. 29, 87th Cong. 1st Sess., 50 (1961).
21. 109 Cong. Rec. 8499–8503 (daily ed. May 20, 1963).
22. Relations Between Church and State, adopted by 175th General Assembly, May 1963, 12–13.
23. 60 Harv. L. Rev. 793, 800 (1947).
24. As quoted in the Providence Journal, October 22, 1962.
25. Howe, review of Stokes, Church and State in the United States, 64 Harv. L. Rev. 170, 174 (1950).
26. *Id.* at 172–73.
27. Murray, *America's Four Conspiracies,* in Cogley, ed., Religion in America 12 (1958).

28. Nichols, Religion and Education in a Free Society, *id*. at 162–63.
29. The Catholic Messenger (Davenport, Iowa) January 10, 1963, p. 1.
30. Church and State, January 1963, p. 14.
31. I was later enabled to verify the quotations when the Rev. Robert C. Hartnett, S.J., succeeded in having a copy sent to me from Rome. Msgr. Booth's book is a doctoral dissertation.
32. Murray, *Governmental Repression of Heresy*, The Catholic Theological Society of America, Proceedings of the Third Annual Meeting 26, 90 (1948).
33. Murray, *Contemporary Orientations of Catholic Thought on Church and State in the Light of History*, 10 Theological Studies 177, 227 (1949).
34. Quoted in A. F. Carrillo de Albornoz, Roman Catholicism and Religious Liberty 34–35 (World Council of Churches, Geneva, 1959).
35. Hocking, *The Principles of Religious Liberty*, 20 Int'l. Rev. of Missions 493, 500–501 (1931).

EPILOGUE: NEUTRALITY AS OF JUNE 1963

1. School District of Abington Township v. Schempp, 374 U.S. 203 (1963).
2. Sherbert v. Verner, 374 U.S. 398 (1963).
3. School District of Abington Township v. Schempp, 374 U.S. 203, 215 (1963).
4. *Id*. at 222.
5. *Id*. at 218.
6. *Id*. at 225–226.
7. *Id*. at 222.
8. *Id*. at 217.

9. *Id.* at 219.
10. *Id.* at 220.
11. *Id.* at 306.
12. *Id.* at 299.
13. *Id.* at 246.
14. *Id.* at 317.
15. *Id.* at 318.
16. *Id.* at 320, n. 8.
17. *Id.* at 222.
18. *Id.* at 224-225.
19. *Id.* at 225.
20. *Id.* at 306.
21. *Id.* at 300–301.
22. *Id.* at 301.
23. The Wall Street Journal, June 19, 1963, 12.
24. Time Magazine, June 28, 1963, 14.
25. School District of Abington Township v. Schempp, 374 U.S. 203, 299 (1963).
26. Sherbert v. Verner, 374 U.S. 398, 400 (1963).
27. *Id.* at 422.
28. Braunfeld v. Brown, 366 U.S. 599 (1961).
29. Sherbert v. Verner, 374 U.S. 398, 415–416 (1963).
30. Engel v. Vitale, 370 U.S. 421, 437 (1962).
31. School District of Abington Township v. Schempp, 374 U.S. 203, 229 (1963).
32. Sherbert v. Verner, 374 U.S. 398, 412 (1963).
33. School District of Abington Township v. Schempp, 374 U.S. 203, 295 (1963).
34. *Id.* at 301–302.
35. *Id.* at 317.
36. Kurland, *The School Prayer Cases*, in Oaks, ed., The Wall between Church and State 142, 178–79 (1963).

PUBLISHED ROSENTHAL
LECTURES 1948–1964

1948 Hazard, John N. "The Soviet Union and International Law," *Illinois Law Review*, XLIII, 591.

1949 Freund, Paul A. *On Understanding the Supreme Court.* Boston: Little, Brown & Co.

1951 Dawson, John P. *Unjust Enrichment, A Comparative Analysis.* Boston: Little, Brown & Co.

1952 Feller, Abraham H. *United Nations and World Community.* Boston: Little, Brown & Co.

1952 Horsky, Charles A. *The Washington Lawyer.* Boston: Little, Brown & Co.

1953 Vanderbilt, Arthur T. "The Essentials of A Sound Judicial System," *Northwestern University Law Review*, XLVIII.

1954 Berle, Adolf A., Jr. *The Twentieth Century Capitalist Revolution.* New York: Harcourt, Brace.

1956 Hurst, James W. *Law and the Conditions of Freedom in the Nineteenth Century United States.* Madison: University of Wisconsin Press.

1956 Sohn, Louis B. "United Nations Charter Revision and the Rule of Law: A Program for Peace," *Northwestern University Law Review*, L, 709.

1956   Gross, Ernest A. "Major Problems in Disarmament," *Northwestern University Law Review*, LI, 299.

1956   Parker, John J. "Dual Sovereignty and the Federal Courts," *Northwestern University Law Review*, LI, 407.

1957   Ukai, Nobushige. "The Individual and the Rule of Law Under the New Japanese Constitution," *Northwestern University Law Review*, LI, 733.

1957   Papale, Antonia Edward. "Judicial Enforcement of Desegregation: Its Problems and Limitations," *Northwestern University Law Review*, LII, 301.

1957   Hart, Herbert L.A. "Murder and the Principles of Punishment: England and the United States," *Northwestern University Law Review*, LII, 433.

1958   Green, Leon. *Traffic Victims: Tort Law and Insurance*. Evanston, Ill.: Northwestern University Press.

1960   Radcliffe, Cyril John. *The Law and Its Compass*. Evanston, Ill.: Northwestern University Press.

1961   Eisenstein, Louis. *The Ideologies of Taxation*. New York: Ronald Press.

1961   Havighurst, Harold C. *The Nature of Private Contract*. Evanston, Ill.: Northwestern University Press.

1962   Pike, James Albert. *Beyond the Law:* the religious and ethical meaning of the lawyer's vocation. New York: Doubleday and Co.

1964   Katz, Wilber G. *Religion and American Constitutions*. Evanston, Ill.: Northwestern University Press.

A NOTE ON MANUFACTURE

THE TEXT OF THIS BOOK was set on the Linotype in a face
called JANSON, an "Old Face" of the Dutch school cut in
Amsterdam by the Hungarian, Nicholas Kis, *circa* 1690.
Janson's authorship was long attributed erroneously to An-
ton Janson, a Hollander who had been employed in Leipzig
where the matrices were re-discovered. These same mats are
today in the possession of the Stempel foundry, Frankfurt,
and the machine-cast version you are reading was modelled
directly on type produced from the original strikes.

The book was composed, printed, and bound by KINGS-
PORT PRESS, INC., Kingsport, Tennessee. WARREN PAPER
COMPANY manufactured the paper. The typography and
binding designs are by *Guy Fleming*.